# Self-Leadership

# Self-Leadership

How to Become a More
Successful, Efficient, and
Effective Leader
from the Inside Out

## ANDREW BRYANT
## ANA LUCIA KAZAN

NEW YORK   CHICAGO   SAN FRANCISCO
LISBON   LONDON   MADRID   MEXICO CITY   MILAN
NEW DELHI   SAN JUAN   SEOUL   SINGAPORE
SYDNEY   TORONTO

The **McGraw·Hill** Companies

1 2 3 4 5 6 7 8 9 0   DOC/DOC   1 8 7 6 5 4 3 2 1

ISBN  978-0-07-179909-6
MHID  0-07-179909-5

e-ISBN  978-0-07-179910-2
e-MHID  0-07-179910-9

McGraw-Hill books are available at special quantity discounts to use as premiums and sales promotions or for use in corporate training programs. To contact a representative, please e-mail us at bulksales@mcgraw-hill.com.

This book is printed on acid-free paper.

Library of Congress Cataloging-in-Publication Data

Bryant, Andrew.
   Self-leadership : how to become a more successful, efficient, and effective leader from the inside out / by Andrew Bryant and Ana Lucia Kazan.
      p. cm.
   Includes bibliographical references and index.
   ISBN-13: 978-0-07-179909-6 (alk. paper)
   ISBN-10: 0-07-179909-5 (alk. paper)
   1. Leadership—Psychological aspects. 2. Self-perception. 3. Self-esteem.
I. Kazan, Ana Lucia. II. Title.
   BF637.L4B79 2012
   158'.4—dc23

                                                      2012016984

*Andrew Bryant dedicates this book to his wife, who has known him at his best and at his worst: "Zurina, you are my inspiration to walk my talk and be the best that I can be."*

*Ana Kazan dedicates this book to Juliana and Samir, the "country" where her soul truly belongs; to Gael, our new little gift from God, and to Luciana, who made him possible; to dad Eudes; and to Badri, the rock we all can trust.*

# Contents

# Preface

This book is the result of a collaboration of two people interested in the same topic but from different backgrounds, from countries on opposite sides of the globe, and who have never physically met (at the time of writing).

The topic is self-leadership, which is the ability to influence yourself to think and behave in ways that are consistent with who you are and are conducive to the pursuit of goals and experiences that are important and relevant to you. Self-leadership requires (and helps you to get) that you have an idea of where you are going, so that everything else—your thoughts and actions—can serve that (or those) objective(s). With a toolbox composed of carefully designed strategies to keep you on track, self-leadership puts you on the path to live a more purposeful and fulfilling life, liberated from vain pursuits and worries, focusing on the one person whom you can really change in life—you—and by doing so, becoming someone who can influence others.

Self-leadership is important for individuals because it allows them to live more authentic and fulfilling lives; it is also important to organizations because self-leaders are more motivated, productive, and creative.

The two people who have never met in person are a Brazilian-born woman, currently living in the United States, Ana Lucia Kazan, PhD, and an English-born man, living in Singapore, Andrew Bryant, CSP, PCC.

This collaboration started in 2009. Ana was searching self-leadership on the web and came across Self Leadership International's website (http://www.selfleadership.com/). Ana e-mailed Andrew, the founder of the company, and they set up the first of many Skype calls. On one of these calls the idea of the book came up, and you are reading the manifestation of this idea.

When she first made contact with Andrew, Ana had just returned to Brazil after living in the United States for 15 years. She attended Ohio State University (OSU) graduate school, getting her master's and then her doctorate working as a researcher for the OSU Leadership Center, the OSU Medical Center, Nationwide Enterprise, and Lehigh Carbon Community College. Reestablishing her roots in Brazil, she was starting her consulting business on research and adult education, with an emphasis on self-leadership, and she wanted to see what other self-leadership entrepreneurial initiatives were happening around the world.

Andrew Bryant, self-described as English by birth, Australian by choice, and Singaporean by residence, founded Self Leadership International as a boutique leadership consulting company in Australia in 1999. His methodology was based on his years of study and practice of topics that included physiotherapy, acupuncture, hypnosis, Neuro-Linguistic Programming neuro-semantics, hypnosis, coaching, business, and leadership. This eclectic fusion gave him the ability to look at improving human performance by looking at the individual, the group, and the organization and find the leverage point for change. He moved the company's headquarters to Singapore in 2004 after doing extensive work with Singapore Airlines and seeing the need for leadership and the growth in the Asian market.

The move has been fruitful, and as a Certified Professional Speaker (CSP) and Professional Certified Coach (PCC) Andrew is highly sought after by companies that want to develop their leaders and leadership culture. He is known for his ability to inspire people and likes blending constructive realism with humor to entertain and engage his worldwide audiences.

During e-mail exchanges and Skype calls, Ana and Andrew explored their belief and understanding that self-leadership was a valuable approach and toolkit that could help individuals and organizations improve the quality of their lives and work. Both passionately embraced the ethics of self-leadership, an approach to life that's about responsibility for one's own thinking, feeling, actions, and results. They shared the understanding that self-leadership, unlike some leadership theories, was not prescriptive—in other words, it doesn't dictate what people should see, know, and do. Self-leadership is a journey, a daily practice that is powerful regardless of where you are in your life.

This book was written to provide you with tools and insights about how we, as humans, think, feel, view the world, make decisions, set goals, relate to others, and receive feedback. Once you have these insights in hand, we, the authors, then share with you the self-leadership path, which we both believe you should be ready to take, since this book attracted you.

We hope you will read the book, write in it, use it as a workbook, and most importantly practice or refine your own self-leadership, regardless of what is going on around you.

For Ana and for Andrew, awareness of self-leadership has been a strong influence in their lives. Ana started practicing self-leadership before even knowing about the concept. A former journalist, she radically changed her life when moving to the United States, with the dream of pursuing her master's degree in communication. Previously diagnosed with attention deficit disorder (ADD), Ana had to learn by herself how to overcome and improve her life path by taking realistic and committed responsibility for her actions, monitoring herself and self-correcting her own thoughts, behaviors, and actions in order to pursue her dreams in the United States. Under the influence of great leaders, among whom was team leader Dr. Garee W. Earnest of the OSU Leadership Center, Ana came into contact with all leadership theories, including those started at that very own Ohio State. At the time of her doctoral studies, while working with Dr. Earnest, Ana found a first article about self-leadership, seeing in it an explanation for how her own trajectory in life had unfolded. The year was 1996, and since then Ana has been practicing, researching, and teaching self-leadership in Brazil and the United States. At the time this book is released, Ana will have just finished her postdoctoral research on international self-leadership at North Carolina State University, with Dr. R. Dale Safrit.

Andrew believes that "we teach best what we most need to learn," and he has honed his self-leadership through building businesses, losing businesses, founding companies, and sharing relationships, some that worked and some that didn't. He has taught and coached thousands of people to live and work more effectively using these tools, but most importantly he continues to work on himself to be a better man.

During the writing of this book, Andrew and Ana connected with Dr. Jeff Houghton and Dr. Christopher Neck, worldwide renowned self-leadership researchers who, along with Charles Manz, defined and diffused self-leadership in academic and popular settings all over the world. Through collaboration with Drs. Houghton and Neck the Revised Self-leadership Questionnaire is now available to you, for free (we will provide you with a link in Chapter 9). In addition to receiving your own, very useful assessment, you will be helping international researchers to understand how self-leadership works across cultures.

This book won't read itself, nor will it do the exercises for you, but if you are ready to take more control of your life, create healthier relationships, live more authentically, or positively influence others, then you have a key in your hands. But be warned: once you know about self-leadership you will never again feel comfortable blaming or complaining, because now you have the power to choose!

# Self-Leadership

## CHAPTER 1

# Why Self-Leadership?

Imagine a large chessboard. Now consider you are a piece on this chessboard. Are you a pawn, moving slowly forward with little choice and at the mercy of other, more powerful pieces? Or are you a knight, able to take risks and attack but with little concern for your own safety? Perhaps you are a bishop, able to move rapidly but constrained to a diagonal path from which you may not deviate. Or you may think of yourself as a rook (i.e., a castle), solid and safe but not very adventurous. A king? He's very important but requires other pieces to serve and defend him. Which leaves the queen, highly flexible, adaptable, and able to move in any direction.

Do you know who you should be?

You should be sick and tired of being a piece of wood and pushed around a board by someone else! In life and in business, before we lead others we must be able to lead ourselves.

This book is about self-leadership, or how you intentionally influence yourself to achieve your objectives. Self-leadership is not for pawns; it is for people who want to choose how they live and work. It is for people who believe—or who always suspected and/ or hoped—that they can live a positive and productive life and influence those around them to do the same.

Self-leadership works, whether you are an employee, manager, teacher, parent, or even someone who currently doesn't want to be defined by what you do. Self-leadership works because it is the foundation for being an effective human being living in a contemporary world. So whether you are reading this book for your own personal and professional development or you are a manager wanting to create an empowered team, practicing self-leadership and encouraging others to live with self-leadership is an important task.

On the business side, self-leadership is important as a foundation for personal, team, business, and strategic leadership (see Figure 1.1), and it is a starting point for any organizational or leadership development program (see Chapter 9).

To be a leader you must be able to think effectively, behave congruently, and relate empathetically. The authors' research and experience shows that self-leadership is necessary to achieve all

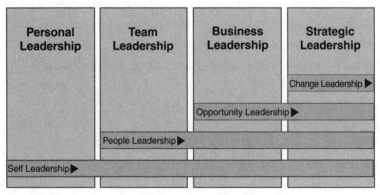

**FIGURE 1.1**   Self-Leadership Forms the Foundation for Effective Leadership.

three of these qualities. As it turns out, these qualities also make anyone a great human being.

With the flattening of hierarchies, the emergence of global teams, and the need for empowered and engaged people and employees everywhere, a new style of leadership is required. Managers and leaders need greater and better self-observation, self-confidence, self-management, and decision-making abilities.

As a practicing self-leader, you can become a competent communicator, able to collaborate with or lead a team, open to learning equally from successes and mistakes, and conversant on how to best utilize your strengths. As a practicing self-leader you will be able to raise awareness of the importance of goals and foster your followers' transcendence of their own interest for the sake of the team or organization. Encouraging self-leadership within a team or organization leads to more collaborative, committed, and engaged employees.

Self-leadership is based in science (see Chapter 12), and the authors have applied the ideas in this book to multinational companies and tested those international professionals' self-leadership. The authors are also sharing in this book a link to the most updated academic self-leadership questionnaire, which can be taken online. Many chapters of this book have practices, which have been tested, to build your self-leadership in a variety of situations.

As humans we face fear and uncertainty at different levels and throughout different phases in our lives. More and more we are coming to the realization that while we go through life's phases we will not have people around to support and encourage us all the time. To successfully navigate and triumph through these challenges we will need to develop our self-observation, self-confidence, self-management, and resilience to become the best we can be, regardless of whether or not we are surrounded by support, or by friendship, or by encouragement.

With self-leadership we can manage stress and achieve peak states of focus and creativity. As we exercise our self-leadership we become a positive force influencing those around us.

Consider Nelson Mandela, a man who was imprisoned 27 years for acting on his beliefs and yet on release chose not to be consumed by anger and hatred but to lead his party (the African National Congress, or ANC) in negotiations that led to a multiracial democracy. During his presidency of South Africa (1994–1999) he often exercised self-leadership in the process of reconciliation. The 2009 movie *Invictus* tells the story of how President Mandela was inspired by a Victorian poem of the same name and how he inspired the captain of the Springbok national rugby team to apply self-leadership to lead his team to victory against all odds.

The last lines of the poem "Invictus" by William Ernest Henley (1849–1903) capture the spirit of self-leadership:

> *It matters not how strait the gate,*
> *How charged with punishments the scroll,*
> *I am the master of my fate:*
> *I am the captain of my soul.*

When you think of a self-leader, who comes to mind for you? While you think about that (it is good when we can have role models, although we cannot always find them), meet a very important self-leader: you!

Research has shown that environmental factors in our early years impact our self-leadership mindset; so if you are born into a family that teaches you cause and effect in a nurturing way and you have the freedom to make choices, then you have been dealt a great hand of cards. As an adult you get to pick up new cards in the form of learning experiences, but ultimately what makes the difference is how you play your cards as you face life's challenges and opportunities.

Is it natural for you to act and live independently and self-reliantly? Maybe you were born with a very independent personality, prone to critical thinking. Or maybe your parents (or family or community) promoted independent thinking and self-reliance.

If you fall in the category above, that's great. You are off to a great start.

But many people were not dealt the same hand of self-leadership cards; they were encouraged instead to consult with family or friends and to be more fearful or cautious with unknown situations. They were given fewer opportunities to *try their hand* at adventurousness. As a result, they became more dependent on the external world, on other people, and so they may prefer not to be exposed to situations in which they have to make decisions and act alone.

Self-leadership can emerge in extreme situations. When facing danger, the individual who previously always hid from trouble may find an inner strength and start to take charge of his or her life. Or under the influence of love or care, someone who has been extremely cautious his whole life may start taking little steps toward independent action. Self-leadership can be revealed through love or through suffering, or yet, as shown in this book, it can emerge from a more measured path to growing ourselves and harnessing our own resilience.

Self-leadership means taking responsibility for our own lives. Some of us had to bravely face life's difficulties alone, while others have been sheltered from the reality that they are responsible for the actions they take. Overcaring parents or a maternal or patriarchal culture or community can breed adults who have been able to avoid responsibility their whole lives.

Before envying such people, remember that they are not living their lives to the fullest. Actually, they are living in a cloud of denial, not exploring great things about themselves and not contributing great things to the world. Coauthor Ana refers to this state, in her classes, as "living in the fog." Many of us go about our whole lives inside this fog of unclarity, half-thought decisions, misunderstandings, and overall confusion about how life really is.

In some ways, it is not easy to learn self-leadership if we don't have people to teach us. Some of us were born to parents who had little or no opportunities to study, travel, and learn about the world. So how could they teach us something they really didn't know very well? In addition to the influence of parents and families, some cultures do not encourage independent thought and action, preferring instead to consist of obedient automatons. But even in such cultures self-leaders emerge and show that having a meaningful and significant life is possible.

An example of such a person is Li Cunxin (pronounced "Lee Schwin Sing") who is a remarkable man with an extraordinary life. In his autobiography *Mao's Last Dancer*, Li recounts his determination, perseverance, vision, courage, hard work, and, in particular, the sacred family values and integrity that he learned in poverty-stricken China, which has driven him to become one of the best dancers in the world. He tells of how he, the sixth of seven sons born to peasants, grew up worshipping Mao Zedong before defecting to the United States. The book and the film depict his struggle to gain independent thinking and action after being programmed to just obey.

Not everybody who learned things the hard way can teach them. It takes a method to teach, an awareness of what is to be learned, and the ability to observe others to know how to present the subject to be learned so as to provide better understanding. It takes time and patience, something that very few people have nowadays, so it's not useful to blame parents, families, communities, or cultures.

Because you are here right now, in this book, you are opening up the self-leadership opportunity in your life, and you are ready to learn. This indicates that you are a true self-leader.

Self-leaders focus on what they can do to be the best they can be. They do so, not because they are competing with others or want to overcome everyone around them, but because they want to focus on being the best they can be; they will also not shy away from helping others. Self-leadership is not selfish. Self-leaders will not take over responsibility for other people's goals or lives, but they will offer empathy, quality attention, and focused effort to help. Self-leaders know that ultimately it is the individual's responsibility to act in his or her own life. So if the other person is not ready, self-leaders respectfully move on to continue their work in their own lives.

It is a misconception that people who are outspoken or express themselves more aggressively are self-leaders. This behavior is not necessarily self-leadership. Self-leadership does not mean stepping on others to make your opinion heard. The fictional, rapacious Gordon Gekko financier in the 1987 movie *Wall Street* is most definitely not a self-leader.

Self-leadership is self-satisfying: self-leaders keep count only to themselves about the steps they have taken toward realizing their own plan. It has nothing to do with forcing their way of being or thinking or acting upon others. When you are a self-leader, it does not matter too much what others do or think. You know your path; you are acting with ethics and honesty, conscious of not hurting anyone with your plan, and you are keeping careful track of your own steps to realize what you want for your life. What others do or think may have an impact on your plans, but what a self-leader does with it is consider it just another challenge to be addressed, a slight change in path to get where she or he needs to be. Self-leaders can also change their goals if they analyze new circumstances. They are autonomous, independent thinkers who can adapt to new situations even if these circumstances were not part of their original plan. Because they count on themselves and are aware of their strengths and weaknesses, they are not afraid of new things. They know they can try on and continue with the new path or return to their preplanned path.

Self-leadership also implies accepting the self-leadership of others and respecting the paths they have chosen for themselves. As self-leaders, we can definitely try to see whether both paths can be complementary and harmonious. If the other person doesn't think it can, the self-leader just proceeds to his or her own path.

The fact that self-leaders have their own goals does not mean that they disregard everybody else's or that they cannot share the goals of a team of which they are a part. On the contrary, self-leaders know the importance of feeling fulfilled and able to find one's own path, so they support others around them in their pursuit of their own path. Because of self-leadership's provided clarity and responsibility, self-leaders understand their role in being ethical, truthful, and responsible to themselves and to their role in the world around them. They also will support and encourage—but not force or impose upon—anyone else to become a self-leader, but they will continue moving forward on their own path. Self-leaders therefore make good mentors because they act as role models for the up and coming.

With a developed sense of responsibility for their own lives, self-leaders know that they only have themselves to blame if they cannot accomplish their goals. Self-leaders are constantly observing their actions, controlling their thoughts, and measuring their achievements against their own benchmarks. They want to do well in relation to their own goals, not to anyone else's. They understand that the best teams are composed of people who are responsible and accountable for their own actions and decisions—people on whom everyone else can count.

An example of someone who lived for someone else's goals and did not take responsibility is the tennis champion Andre Agassi.

Agassi writes in his autobiography about how his father forced him to play tennis for the money and how he turned to crystal meth to escape. Later, with the help of coaching, Agassi learned to love the game for his own reasons and found a purpose in raising tens of millions of dollars for at-risk youth in his hometown of Las Vegas, where he opened a preparatory academy.

A self-leader's goal is to feel accomplished with oneself, independently of what life has handed him or her. Not all self-leaders want to be world-famous, have fabulous riches, or hold the most prestigious jobs. Some people may just dream of being calmer, being able to focus on their classes at school, finishing a degree, or becoming a better parent. These are as much a self-leader's goals as are being able to control his or her finances or manage a company's budget. In other words, what motivates self-leaders are not necessarily grandiose goals or accomplishments; it could be something deeper, more intrinsic.

As a personal example, coauthor Ana was once diagnosed with attention deficit disorder (ADD). Indeed, for many years she had trouble finishing many of the projects she started. Although she was an accomplished journalist, she had to work very hard to overcome boredom and lack of interest in small, repetitive tasks and in long conversations. She would engage in myriad activities, finish only a few, have difficulty relaxing, and constantly be in a hurry, running from place to place, to make life somewhat meaningful. She observes: "I had so many minor car accidents, all due to constantly being in a hurry and distracted while driving."

All these activities and distractions, within the scenario of ADD, ended up causing a major breakthrough in her life. She got involved with the wrong type of people (but was too busy and enchanted with everything else that she did to really notice that), let go of caution, and literally lost everything that she had. It took this formidable loss, a move to another country, and a restart in life totally on her own, to help her overcome her ADD with a strong sense of responsibility, self-observation, self-reliance, and self-accountability. She began practicing self-leadership long before knowing what it was. "Self-leadership helped me have a second chance in life," says Ana.

Self-leadership is also the ability to conduct ourselves in a responsible, accountable manner, centered on doing what we know is good for us and that won't damage others. At the same time, self-leadership is a way to contribute to the world by carrying our own weight, by being responsible at least for ourselves, but optimally, helping to inspire others into being accountable for themselves as well. We can contribute to the world by knowing our own strengths and weaknesses, using these strengths to overcome the weaknesses, and just getting to be better human beings. A self-leader is someone who does not hinder efforts but contributes; who finds where and when one's contribution is needed; and who knows that he or she may not be able to change the world but can surely change himself or herself into a better being. This is plenty of work for a lifetime.

An important distinction with self-leadership is that the self-leader does not necessarily have to be a "leader" in the traditional meaning of the term. Leading others is not something that everybody likes to do; some people like to follow. The world needs both leaders and followers. Leaders open the path; followers pave and stabilize it. It is a great thing when leaders and followers are both self-leaders. In such a situation, everyone knows her or his role and what she or he is good at. There should not to be a dispute about someone taking the role or the merits of another, as everybody would be satisfied just being the best they could be. Everyone has distinct abilities; we don't all need to be the same thing. So, learning self-leadership means, first and foremost, knowing ourselves, being aware of our own strengths and weaknesses, finding opportunities to grow, and recognizing threats to our own paths where we are likely to fall. Self-leadership, indeed, starts with self-observation, and this topic is what the next chapter explores.

## Summary of the Chapter

Self-leadership is the learned ability to intentionally influence ourselves to achieve our objectives; it is the foundation of personal, team, business, and strategic leadership. Self-leadership is a learnable science-based competence that helps its practitioners become better communicators, team collaborators, and leaders of teams; be able to learn equally from successes and mistakes; and become conversant on how to best utilize our own strengths. Self-leaders are effective at deciding on and reaching personal and professional goals, and they also inspire others to transcend in their own personal and professional lives. People are different from one another: some of us may have degrees of self-leadership, and others don't. Wherever your self-leadership level is or isn't, it can be improved. Encouraging self-leadership within a team or organization leads to more collaborative, committed, and engaged employees.

## CHAPTER 2

# What Is Self-Leadership?

*Mastering others is strength.*
*Mastering yourself is true power.*
—Lao Tzu

We define self-leadership as the practice of intentionally influencing our thinking, feeling, and behaviors to achieve our objectives. Simply put, self-leadership emerges from self-awareness, which leads to greater self-responsibility and behavioral flexibility, which in turn increases our ability to reach our goals. Becoming a self-leader and maintaining self-leadership is a self-development activity, but organizations that encourage self-leadership reap the benefit (see Table 2.1).

The authors propose that self-leadership be the foundation of any organizational development or program. To skip the self-leadership piece is to leave out a significant part of the puzzle of developing a learning organization.

This chapter takes a look at the origins of self-leadership and outlines some of its components, specifically, self-management, self-monitoring, self-motivation, self-confidence (overcoming self-sabotage), resilience, optimism, and decision making.

**TABLE 2.1**  Personal and Organizational Benefits of
Self-Leadership

| Personal Benefits of Self-Leadership | Organizational Benefits of Self-Leadership |
|---|---|
| Self-awareness | Engaged and empowered workforce |
| Self-confidence | |
| Finding meaning and purpose | Improved goal setting and results |
| Decreased stress | Faster and better decision making |
| Increased happiness | More creativity and innovation |
| Better relationships | Reduced conflicts |
| | Collaborative team efforts |

## THE SIMPLICITY OF SELF-MANAGEMENT

The modern concept of self-leadership evolved from studies about self-management during the 1980s, when American companies started implementing telecommuting work teams in some areas and circumstances. At that time, self-management studies targeted the ability to manage a person's own time and efficacy, without the control and observation of managers or colleagues, while working away from the office environment. Good self-management includes abilities such as goal setting, decision making, focusing, planning, scheduling, task tracking, self-evaluation, self-intervention, and self-development. Interestingly, the birth of the concept of self-management came from the field of medicine. In medicine, self-management is related to the education of patients with chronic conditions (e.g., diabetes, arthritis, heart disease, and asthma) to keep their conditions under control through the practice of healthy behaviors. By taking responsibility for the day-to-day management of their diseases, patients become more knowledgeable and feel more confident about their ability to lead a better quality life, utilizing fewer healthcare resources.

In the context of corporations, self-management is related to the ability to control a person's own disruptive impulses; to work with transparency (i.e., with openness and integrity); to work consciously, which means taking the responsibility of managing oneself; to be adaptable and flexible with changing situations; to have a drive to personal excellence, for achievement; and to have initiative, or readiness to act when needed. While self-leadership incorporates self-management, it is more than that. Self-management targets professional outcomes and efficiency, and so it is externally motivated; self-leadership, on the other hand, is a broader self-influence, aimed also at personal fulfillment and including self-motivational cognitive, behavioral, and mental strategies that put us in the best state to achieve personal efficacy in the contexts of our choosing.

As a personal example, coauthor Andrew was coaching an entrepreneurial CEO who was struggling with his emotional outbursts and his communication with his team. This CEO quickly grasped and applied the principles we are sharing in this book; he said:

> *Self-leadership has produced results for me that I had no idea were possible. In 12 months I have grown enormously as an executive: my relations with managers and staff are far more harmonious; I have been able to coach my team through significant personal development; I am more understanding and accepting of my broader responsibilities as a leader; I have much more energy and am able to motivate myself more easily. Most importantly, I have grown my company's revenues and profits significantly.*
>
> —Grant Halloran,
> CEO and cofounder of Orbis

Manz (1986) was the first to define modern self-leadership. He described self-leadership as a journey to self-discovery and self-satisfaction, a method of self-influence, a technique for self-efficacy, a source of behavioral control, and even a process of self-fulfillment. Manz's studies were based on social learning theory, on Bandura's 1971 social cognitive theory, Snyder's (1974, 1979) self-monitoring studies, Deci and Ryan's (1985) self-motivation studies, and Burns's (1980) cognitive therapy.

## SELF-MONITORING: THE NEW BEHAVIORAL TO-DO

Social learning theory asserts that human beings learn their basic modes of behaving from social situations and obtain satisfaction to their needs only through their contact with other people (Rotter 1954). The theory looks at how the expectation of social group reinforcement can determine and predict behaviors as well as how it is the social context that determines what is individually desirable or not. Simply put, we take our behavioral cues from those around us. We can observe this when new people join a team; they quickly adopt the behavioral norms of that team or risk being ostracized.

Bandura (1986) developed social learning theory into social cognitive theory by examining self-regulatory processes. He said that people seek reciprocity between their behavior and environmental factors—that is, people will have a higher motivation to learn if results of that learning will be positively appreciated by their surrounding social group. Bandura also said that people learn behaviors and consequences of behaviors vicariously, by simply observing environmental cues and behaviors modeled by people around them, assessing their performance through this dynamic. According to Bandura, we also learn from observing the group's reaction to other people's behavior. This knowledge is essential if we are going to create self-leadership cultures (see Chapter 9), because self-leaders are aware of environmental cues and act upon them.

Obviously, trying to fit in is a natural behavior. Self-leadership brings awareness to this process (i.e., self-monitoring) so that we notice cues from our surrounding social environment and are aware of the reactions to and consequences of our own behavior on any group that is important to us (Gardner and Cole 1988).

Consider some of the groups to which you belong, your team or work group, a sports team or parents group. What are some of the behaviors that you have adopted from that group? We have provided Table 2.2 for you to write down your reflections.

As a personal example, Andrew moved from England to Australia when he was 25 years old; here's what he observed about his behavior with new groups:

> In Australia I took up surfing and soon found my English accent and mannerisms were a source of ridicule amongst the "Aussie" surfers. I quickly adapted my speech patterns and behaviors to "fit in" so that I could enjoy the surfing. In this case I chose to adapt but this does not mean I choose to fit in to every group, nor should you.

People who are extremely high self-monitors can be overly self-conscious and self-judging; on the other hand if you are oblivious to the effect of your behaviors, you will run into difficulties.

**TABLE 2.2**  Group Behaviors That I Have Adopted

| Group | Behavior |
|---|---|
|  |  |
|  |  |
|  |  |

As a self-leader you will be able to notice the so-called rules of the game in any social situation and choose whether or not to play; this allows you to be perceived as being "authentic."

## BUILDING SELF-CONFIDENCE

Self-leadership is grounded in self-confidence. Self-confidence is the confidence on one's own personal judgment, ability, and power; as the famous Henry Ford quote goes: "Whether you think you can or think you can't—you are right."

Research (Sears 1990) shows that poise and communication skills are more important than all the other factors in people being perceived as self-confident. Whatever your political views, we think you will agree that poise and communication skills helped Barack Obama become President Obama.

Bandura (1977) linked self-confidence with self-efficacy. Self-leadership promotes self-confidence because it increases individuals' self-knowledge and self-awareness, and along with it comes the ability to predict personal behavior and thus control it when needed or wanted. The practice of self-leadership builds self-confidence and helps to avoid the danger of becoming overconfident, which comes from avoiding information that could threaten our self-image (Benabou and Tirole 2002). This is because the self-leader has a healthy relationship to feedback, self-observation, and self-evaluation. Self-knowledge, which builds upon control of personal behavior along with an appreciation for feedback, self-observation, and self-evaluation, brings with it self-efficacy, closing the cycle theorized by Bandura (1977).

## THE GREAT POSSIBILITIES OF SELF-MOTIVATION

Self-motivation is another intrinsic component of self-leadership, one that implies the ability to stay focused, enthused, and motivated about one's own goals (Edic 1997). Spitzer (1995) defined self-motivation as the "real motivation"—that is, motivation that is internally borne, moved by strong inner desires. External motivation, such as a pep talk or motivational seminar, is a bit like showering—you smell good for a while, but the effect wears off.

As humans we are driven by desires (Spitzer 1995)—so, just as an exercise, review the following list and determine what drives you (check all that apply).

☐ The desire for activity

☐ The desire for ownership

☐ The desire for power

☐ The desire for affiliation

☐ The desire for competence

☐ The desire for achievement

☐ The desire for recognition

☐ The desire for meaning

At the core, all these desires aim at increasing individuals' ability to establish competence and self-determination (Deci and Ryan 1985)—in other words, the autonomy to successfully navigate the environment in which we find ourselves.

Self-leadership is fueled by self-motivation, as the self-leader moves toward obtaining his or her life's goals. More often than not, success means enduring difficulties and setbacks in our plans. This is when self-motivation (i.e., the connection with our inner desires) feeds our individual capacity for persistence and focus, thus fostering efficacy in staying on target, dealing with our environment, or surrounding ourselves with a group of people to achieve our goals. Self-leadership strategies (see Chapter 8) help people stay in constant connection with their inner desires and/or tap into that source of self-motivation, to keep their pace and energy in successfully pursuing their goals.

Chapter 3 deals with the development of the "self" and how we create resourceful or unresourceful mental maps about ourselves and our relationships with others. You can develop self-leadership by yourself or through coaching, but sometimes people need therapy to overcome distorted thinking patterns. Cognitive therapy (also known as "cognitive behavior therapy," or "CBT") integrates

**TABLE 2.3**   Common Distorted Thinking Patterns

| | |
|---|---|
| "Should"ing or "Must"ing | Constantly saying you "should" do something or "must" do something, which indicates that your actions are controlled by something or someone else. |
| Overgeneralizing | When something bad happens, you make it about everything rather than just the thing that happened. For example: "Now *everything* is ruined!" |
| Catastrophizing | Turning everything into a catastrophe and focusing only on the negative. |
| Blaming | Shifting your responsibility to someone or something else. This prevents you from taking action to effect a positive change. |
| Discounting | Not counting positive information or rejecting possible solutions, as in, "That doesn't count" or, "It could have been better." |

self-leadership studies with its unique approach to problem solving. Cognitive therapy (CT) was developed in the 1960s by Dr. Aaron T. Beck, based on the premise that the way we perceive situations influences how we feel emotionally about the situations. So it is not the situation per se that directly affects how a person feels emotionally but rather her or his thoughts about that situation. When people are in distress, they often do not think clearly and their thoughts are distorted in some way. Cognitive therapy helps people to identify their distressing thoughts and to evaluate how realistic the thoughts are. Then they learn to change their distorted thinking. When they think more realistically, they feel better. Table 2.3 shows some common distorted thinking patterns. Do you recognize any in yourself?

Recognizing one's own distortive thinking patterns is a great start for self-leadership practice. By practicing this recognition, eventually you will be able to catch the distortion before it ruins a situation, a relationship, or even parts of your life.

## RESILIENCE: THE ABILITY TO BOUNCE BACK

Self-leadership techniques, like cognitive therapy, enhance thought control, helping people identify defeating thoughts and develop new thoughts to substitute those that are harmful for personal success. Self-leadership stimulates the examination of the accuracy of one's own thoughts and beliefs regarding oneself and any problematic situation at hand.

For example, examine yourself and ask: "Have I failed at something?" "How do I feel about that?" "What does it mean to me?"

For some people a failure is final; they create a catastrophe out of the failure and allow it to define them. The self-leader, on the other hand, steps back from the failure and frames it as a learning experience, adjusting her thinking and behavior to move on, to overcome the difficult experience.

> *Ever tried. Ever failed. No matter. Try again. Fail again.*
> *Fail better.*
>
> —SAMUEL BECKETT,
> IRISH PLAYWRIGHT AND NOBEL PRIZE WINNER

Self-leaders are resilient and are strengthened from difficult experiences. The term *resilience* comes from the field of physics, meaning the quality or property of some materials to quickly recover the original shape or conditions after being pulled, pressed, crushed, and otherwise distorted (Hornby and Ruse 1986). *Resilience* does not mean *invulnerability*; rather, it means having the flexibility to respond to changing situational demands (Block and Block 1980; Block and Kremen 1996; Lazarus, 1993a). Resilient people are able to experience positive emotions even in the midst of stressful events (Tugade, Fredrickson, and Barrett 2006). The use of positive emotions is linked to the ability to cope with difficulties (being resilient), and there is an indication that people who are able to experience positive emotions even during crises are also those who represent positive emotional experiences with precision and specificity (rather than as global pleasant states). They are able to deconstruct their life experiences into distinguishing details and can use this ability to distinguish how parts of whole events can help them identify, in difficult times, those moments that are really negative from those that are positive.

An inspiring example is Terry Fox, the long-distance runner and basketball player who had his leg amputated in 1977 after he was diagnosed with osteosarcoma. With the help of an artificial leg, Fox was walking three weeks after the amputation. He then progressed to playing golf with his father. Doctors were impressed with Fox's positive outlook, stating it contributed to his rapid recovery. He endured 16 months of chemotherapy and ended his treatment with new purpose: he felt he owed his survival to medical advances and wished to live his life in a way that would help others find the same courage he found. To fulfill that purpose, in 1980, with his artificial leg, he embarked on a cross-Canada run to raise money and awareness for cancer research.

Self-leadership strategies help us examine occurring thoughts for their helpfulness or harmfulness, and examine our beliefs and challenge their veracity, substituting the defeating ones with more useful, operative ones. These self-leadership practices help to develop resilience skills. By learning, practicing, and gaining experience in controlling our behaviors and thoughts, we gain resilience to stressful situations.

## REALISTIC OPTIMISM

With resilience, self-leaders have what the authors like to call "realistic optimism." Optimism is the tendency to look to the more favorable side of events or conditions and to expect the most favorable outcome. Realistic optimism is the acceptance that both good and bad things do happen but we can make "good" in either of these circumstances. *Good* in this context means that we can survive whatever it is that life throws at us, learn from those things, and grow. When you practice self-leadership on a daily basis you take a leap of faith and believe that you can learn some things with whatever challenge you face. For self-leaders, every victory, however small, counts. They use life's lessons and experiences to continually build their self-efficacy. The world is a school to self-learners, and they are engaged students.

Take a moment to reflect:

1. What positive lessons has life taught you so far?

2. What do you still need to learn?

## POWERFUL DECISION MAKING

Fundamentally, self-leadership is about choice. With an enhanced self-awareness and an understanding of how we operate in the world—things that the practice of self-leadership brings—we can make better decisions, assertively communicate those decisions, and receive feedback from the results of our decisions.

To do this requires courage and the commitment to practice stepping outside of our comfort zones, to try a new behavior, a new level of assertiveness, and, if it works, try again, and again, perfecting it with each practice. Does it get to a point when we know everything we need to? It doesn't, at least not in the authors' experience. Life has a way of always presenting new situations, new dogmas, and new puzzles to be solved or resolved. Often we don't have the knowledge, experience, or insight to decide on a solution immediately.

Practicing self-leaders can stand the discomfort of not knowing and take the time to think through the challenge. They know that they have the "equipment" needed to think through anything, to theorize and look for information. Self-leaders have initiative and take control of their own behavior, which leads them to search for answers to unknown or difficult problems. They choose to make decisions to the best of their ability: consciously, ethically, sustainably, and respectfully toward others.

### Summary of the Chapter

Self-leadership is a process of self-knowledge, self-influence, and self-guidance that works for the practitioner as well as to the others around him or her. It is an empowering ability that adds insight, thoughtfulness, responsibility, accountability, and confidence to those who choose to practice it.

As you read through the following chapters, we hope that more aspects and benefits of self-leadership will reveal themselves to your understanding. At the end of this book, you can take the self-leadership assessment, by Houghton and Neck, and get your own report to help you get situated about where you are in your own self-leadership journey.

We, the authors, are on the self-leadership journey, and we found it so valuable that we proposed to write this book in a very unlikely partnership, across oceans and continents, a distance of exactly 10,044 miles (16,164 kilometers, or 8,728 nautical miles, since Ana Lucia Kazan lives in Brazil and Andrew Bryant lives in Singapore).

We both owe this book to our choice to practice self-leadership.

# Driver or Passenger?

*Rule your mind or it will rule you.*
—HORACE

John's parents migrated to Australia from central Europe when he was just two years old. They had no friends in their new land, and so when they were warmly welcomed by a religious community they chose to ignore its cultlike culture. John grew up in a strict regime. He was told what was right and wrong and that the ultimate punishment was to be banished from the community. John always felt constricted by the rules and was often in trouble for small misdemeanors. He was told he was stupid, but that assessment just didn't seem right to him. In his midteens, John began to exert his independence by challenging the culture's taboos. At 17 he started to smoke, which was absolutely forbidden, and he was told that unless he stopped he would be expelled. To John's mind this was an opportunity to finally escape and so he continued to smoke, not anticipating the cost.

The community expelled John, forbidding him to return or ever to see his parents again. His newfound freedom came at a huge price: the smothering community had not allowed John to fully develop his identity and his ability to make decisions. For his entire life he had been told what to think and feel; now, without that support system, his world came crashing down. John spent the next 10 years in and out of mental institutions and then 7 more under the care of therapists.

When coauthor Andrew met John, he was functioning way below his potential, working in a store at a golf club. There is a happy ending to this story, but before we share it, let us look at how our sense of self is formed and how we exercise our autonomy (i.e., our decision-making ability).

## THE FORMATION OF OUR SENSE OF SELF

It is interesting that we are not born with a sense of self; it develops as we begin to ask ourselves question such as:

- "Who am I?"

- "What am I?"

- "Am I loved?"

- "What can I do?"

- "What am I good at?"

- "What is my nature, purpose, and destiny?"

- "What is right and wrong?"

The self is formed during our first three years of life as a result of everything that occurs between ourselves and our primary caregivers, whomever they may be. If that relationship is a nurturing one, the self develops in healthy ways; otherwise it will develop maladaptive behaviors. In his book *The Developing Mind: How Relationships and the Brain Interact to Shape Who We Are*, the pediatrician and researcher Daniel Siegel observed that given our estimated total number of neurons (100 billion), each of them with an average of 10,000 direct connections to other neurons, the activation of only one neuron will have a tremendously large impact in several and unexpected areas of our brain.

The type of interactions between parents and their children during the first three years of life determines the patterns of connections of these million billion neurons, thus determining individual patterns of emotional, social, and intellectual brain activity as well. According to Siegel, it is clear that healthy individuals start from healthy attachments with their primary adult caregivers. Emotionally healthy adults foster emotionally healthy children.

The contrary is also true. Emotionally immature and weak parents foster children with a weak sense of self. Children who have little or no interaction with healthy attachment figures lack the right connections for social connectedness, empathy, safety, and trust, thus suffering significant and long-term loss of the capacity to establish intimate interpersonal relationships throughout their lives. Once self/other patterns are established, whether they are healthy ones or not, they influence all later interpersonal relationships. This means that people tend to search for relationships that match the patterns of their early experiences with which they are familiar. People who were overly dependent or overly detached, or those who were physically abused or sexually molested during childhood, may unconsciously repeat these patterns throughout their lives.

Reflect for a moment:

1. Have you adopted a behavior pattern or patterns from one or both of your parents?

2. Are these behaviors under your control, or do they seem to operate automatically?

Studying the development of children during their early years, psychiatrist Margaret Mahler identified different stages we all go through during our first three years of life, progressing from a fusion of identity with the mother to a gradual separation and individuation of identity. Adults are trusted to respond appropriately to children's needs during this time, not neglecting, scolding, yelling, or abandoning them. Struggling with a natural ambivalence during this time, torn between enjoying separate states of independence and dependence, children need to be helped through this struggle by understanding parents. Healthy adults serve as approving mirrors for the child's developing sense of self, optimally leading their children to develop healthy self-esteem and independence.

With unresponsive parents, on the other hand, children develop a sense of insecurity, fail to fully differentiate themselves from their parents, and/or lack the ability to find good role models or feel pride in their accomplishments. They often rebel and feel shame or uncertainty. They typically may suffer later on in life from narcissistic character disorders, such as feelings of grandiosity, an exaggerated sense of self-importance, and an exploitative attitude toward others. They could seek undue attention and admiration from others, or they could become self-absorbed and exaggerate their accomplishments. All this serves to mask a frail self-concept and undeveloped sense of self, which can be traced back to weak father and/or mother figures.

Adults' character disorders could also be rooted in the period of separation and individuation during their early years. Immature caregivers unable to tolerate children's natural progression toward independence could thwart or reject those children during their efforts to individuate. Or they may punish their children or withdraw their emotional support from them, contributing to those individuals' strong feelings of confusion, instability, irritability, impulsive anger, and extreme mood shifts, or to other self-destructive acts, extended periods of disillusionment, and occasional periods of euphoria. Later on in life, these could turn into a lack of clear identity, an absence of deep empathy and understanding for others, poor impulse control, and the inability to tolerate anxiety. Does this remind you of anyone you know?

The development of a sense of self-independence from the other is not just a consequence of the way we separate and differentiate ourselves from our first caretakers. It also continues throughout later stages of life: middle childhood, adolescence, young adulthood, middle adulthood, late adulthood, and senior citizens. Children and adults are at their best and healthiest when they feel both independence and attachment, take joy in themselves, and can see the best in each other. They feel a basic security grounded in a sense of authentic freedom, self-sufficiency, and self-esteem. People with a strong sense of self are not compulsively dependent on others; yet, at the same time they do not fear or shy away from closeness and friendships. They control their impulses; understand their values, needs, and desires; and make wise decisions for themselves and for others. They resist peer pressure when it endangers their welfare or inhibits their growth, find wholesome outlets for fulfillment and satisfaction, and think intelligently and rationally about life's everyday challenges. In sum, people with a strong sense of self lead lives that are both self-actualizing and self-transcending.

Siegel was adamant, however, that the brain is plastic—that is, it can rewire itself into new connections, making the scenario above (a perfect one for self-leadership development) possible even at a later age. With self-awareness and self-responsibility we can build self-leadership from a grounded upbringing or we can create a new "imprint" of self-esteem and power up our ability to have healthy relationships with ourselves and others. This is confirmation that change is possible with the right strategies (see Chapter 8).

## SELF-ESTEEM

Self-esteem reflects a person's evaluation or appraisal of his or her own worth or value. Self-esteem is built through the process of valuing *ourselves*. Seeking our value from *others* or from material possessions is a common trap that leads to very unsatisfactory results because, by its very nature, self-esteem can never be achieved by seeking the approval of others or by acquiring things. Many unproductive and self-defeating behaviors emanate from low self-esteem, such as not speaking up or seeking constant validation. Building healthy and unconditional self-esteem is the foundation of self-leadership.

Reflect for a moment; on a scale of 1 to 10, with 10 being high, *what number would you give your self-esteem today?*

If you gave yourself anything less than a 10, you have discounted your value to yourself. The processes we offer as we move on in this book will help you reconsider your self-value and improve your self-esteem.

It's a curious thing that many of us can accept a lot of things in life, such as enduring a rainy day when we wanted it to be cloudless or having a friend postpone an appointment, but we have difficulty accepting ourselves. When was the last time you just accepted yourself for being you? You are unique; nobody can be you; you have nothing more to do than to be you—can you accept that? What would it be like to accept yourself unconditionally?

Now, you may still feel the need to judge or measure yourself by what you do—most of us have been well conditioned to do this by our school system. Stop for a moment and consider a newborn baby. If you have actually been at the birth of your own child, then this exercise will be even more powerful. At the moment of birth, what can this new human being do? The answer is nothing, unless perhaps cry. Having acknowledged that a newborn can do nothing, how much do we value the infant? Answer: hugely. It is impossible to put a price on how much we value a new baby. Understand that you were once a newborn and therefore came into this world with inherent value; what has happened that has caused you to devalue yourself?

Coauthor Andrew has coached many clients who have shared with him the traumatic events that caused them to take an external criterion or measure, apply it to their sense of self, and then draw the erroneous conclusion that "I'm no good." The fundamental but common error is to confuse our actions with who we are.

Everyone has said something or done something that he or she has regretted later, but this does not decrease that individual's value as a person. The past does not equal the future, and we all contain within us the power of choice: the choice to value ourselves and to choose new thoughts, feelings, speech, and behaviors.

The self-esteem process is like showering—you have to do it every day or you start to stink. So we invite you now to accept yourself as separate from your actions. And as you accept that you are a unique human being, perhaps you can start to appreciate the potential that you have. No one can be you like you can. You have a unique contribution to make just by being on the planet at this time.

## BEING AUTHENTIC

Our self-leadership, our authenticity, and our willingness to become a "driver" or "passenger" in life depend on how we answer the self questions mentioned at the beginning of the chapter. And the environment we grow up in will strongly influence the answers at which we arrive.

Drivers and passengers are evident in the workplace; some of us are willing and have the self-confidence to exercise our autonomy (decision making), while others wait to be told what to do for fear of failure or because they have not considered that they can do something.

A senior private banker shared with me an experience that he had: When he got a new boss, the banker asked him whether he liked his people to speak up with ideas or just follow instructions. The boss said that he definitely wanted new ideas, but when this private banker did speak up he was shot down. After two more attempts at speaking up the banker drew the conclusion that autonomy was not appreciated. Whether employees are encouraged to exercise autonomy is driven by the organization's culture and their manager's leadership style (see Chapter 9).

We may be drivers in some areas of our life and passengers in another. Take a moment to reflect on how you are doing; then fill out Table 3.1 with your responses.

**TABLE 3.1**  Driver or Passenger?

|  | Driver? | Passenger? |
|---|---|---|
| With my parents |  |  |
| With my siblings |  |  |
| With my partner or spouse |  |  |
| In my immediate work team |  |  |
| In my organization |  |  |
| With my boss |  |  |
| In my social life |  |  |
| Within clubs and associations |  |  |

Be aware, the problem is not necessarily being a passenger in some of the roles you have in life. There is only a problem if you are not happy being a passenger. As stated in Chapter 1, some people like to lead, and others like to follow. Whatever you do is fine, as long as that is what you want. But if you have been a passenger and would like to be a driver, then self-leadership can help you to get there, to build skills needed, and do so within a framework of personal growth.

Often people complain that their circumstances prevent choice. Viktor Frankl has shown us that this is not the case. Frankl was interned in a Nazi death camp and completely lost his physical freedom, but he realized that whatever was done to him, he still had the power to choose what he thought and felt about his situation. Frankl survived and went on to become the founder of logotherapy. Logotherapy is based on the paradigm that searching for a meaning in life is the primary motivational force in human beings. That meaning becomes an objective reality, which in itself powerfully moves individuals into accomplishing it. He expresses his thinking thus: "Between stimulus and response there is a space. In that space is our power to choose our response. In our response lies our growth and our freedom."

How strong is your ability to choose?

Perhaps you are a manager or leader and want to develop the autonomy of your people. How do you go about doing so?

To develop autonomy, it is important to remember that we, as humans, are powerful. We cannot fly or shoot fire from our eyes as Superman does, but we can *think*, *feel*, and *do*. We have the power of head, heart, and hand. As Stephen Covey talks about in *The Seven Habits of Highly Effective People*, we have the power to be proactive. When we do or say something, we have the power to choose how we do it or how we say it.

Animals react to the world around them in a pattern of stimulus and response, with flight or fight. Remember the famous experiment by Pavlov with his dogs, bells, and food? While study-ing digestive systems, Russian researcher Ivan Pavlov noticed that laboratory dogs salivated when they saw researchers using lab coats, even though food was not in sight; they associated the pres-ence of lab coats with being given food. The experience came to be known as the dogs and bells experiment, because Pavolv further explored the phenomena, adding other elements for triggering the dogs' reactions, including, at some point, bells. After listening to bells every time the food was presented, dogs would salivate just hearing the bells, even when no food was brought. As humans, we can overcome conditioned responses and master what we *think*, how we *feel*, how we *communicate*, and how we *act*. It is with self-leadership that we can exercise the power to choose our response.

With acceptance of this power to choose we can build the "muscle" of our self-leadership by regularly stepping back from the situations we face and asking these questions (see Figure 3.1):

- "What do I think about this?"

- "What do I feel about this?"

- "What do I say about this?"

- "What do I do about this?"

Like building a muscle, building your power to choose in any situation takes commitment and practice, but the payoff is enor-mous, especially if you consider the number of times you have reacted to a situation only to realize later that you got the pro-verbial wrong end of the stick. In addition, immediate reactions can prevent us seeing opportunities when they come in unfamiliar packages.

Andrew's experience provides an example. He watched with interest as his two children learned to swim. As he related: "My

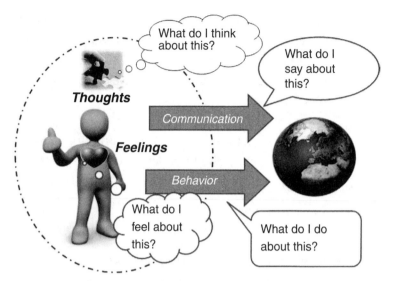

**FIGURE 3.1** A Neuro-Semantic Approach to Self-Leadership. Adapted from L. Michael Hall, Ph.D.

firstborn, Tasha, saw the water and said, 'I don't want to. I don't like it. I can't.' My son Nathan jumped in the water and said, 'I like it' and began to easily move through the new environment."

This example illustrates how confidence in the water is created early in life and self-confidence can generalize to other areas. What is interesting about this example is that although Tasha lacked self-confidence, she was exercising autonomy; she chose to say no to putting her head in the water. The temptation was to force her to do this because as parents we know that learning to swim is important. The outcome of forcing her could be to demonstrate to a five-year-old that her choice doesn't matter and that to exercise it will bring the displeasure of authority figures—her parents.

"The good news," said Andrew, "is that Tasha changed her mind about water and is now swimming well."

We can see from this example that to change behavior we usually have to change how we think and feel about the situation. It is possible, but less likely, that a repeated behavior can change a mindset; for example, a person who hates exercising but persists can learn to love it.

To develop autonomy, and become the driver in your life, practice the following:

1. Own your right to choose. You have a birthright to make choices independently of your upbringing and current culture.

2. Notice your inner dialogue about situations, and quality-control this self-talk. (See the exercise in Chapter 8.)

3. Be aware of how you feel, and realize that these are your emotions and that you have the ability to choose your emotions. (See the exercise in Chapter 4.)

4. Make conscious decisions about what you will say and do, and choose the frame you want to set. (See Chapter 4.)

5. Get feedback on your decisions. Notice the effects of what you say and do, and make adjustments accordingly.

Initially it takes a high degree of self-awareness (i.e., self-monitoring) to run through this process, but with practice it becomes fast and natural.

Remember John, whom we introduced at the beginning of this chapter? Andrew coached John to the awareness that he had the right to choose, and through the coaching John developed a mantra: "It's my life, it's my choice, and I choose."

As John was released from the taboo of making decisions for himself, his confidence grew, and the transformation was spectacular. At work he stepped up from being store man to becoming barman, where he was a hit with his intelligence and wit. He saved his money and traveled from Australia to Vietnam, where he started a business, met his wife, and created the life he chose to live.

## Summary of the Chapter

Are you a driver or a passenger in your life? Our characteristics as adults are developed and learned from childhood and throughout the period of many years because of our parents, families, friends, and experiences. Whatever life has handed you, research shows that the brain is plastic—that is, it can rewire itself into new connections, making it possible for us to develop independence, self-esteem, and self-motivation that we need to become self-leaders even at later ages. With self-awareness and self-responsibility we can build self-leadership from a grounded upbringing or we can create a new imprint of self-esteem and power up our ability to have healthy relationships with ourselves and with others. To change behavior we usually have to change how we think and feel about the situation. To start developing autonomy, start practicing the following:

1. Own your right to choose.

2. Notice and quality-control your inner dialogue about whatever happens to you.

3. Be aware of how you feel, and realize that these are your emotions and you have the ability to choose your emotions.

4. Start practicing making more conscious decisions about what you will say and do in reaction to whatever happens in your life.

5. Start noticing the effects of what you say and do, and make adjustments accordingly.

## CHAPTER 4

# Choices and Decisions

> *It is our choices, Harry,*
> *that show what we truly are,*
> *far more than our abilities.*
>
> —Professor Albus Dumbledore,
> fictional creation of J. K. Rowling

The previous chapter explored our power to choose our thoughts, feelings, communication, and behavior. From our choices come our decisions. Life and work are full of decisions that we must make every day.

Our decisions can be conscious or unconscious. We make choices to meet our human needs, and we make decisions to pursue our intentions, goals, and aspirations. Consciously exercising choice and the ability to make effective decisions is the mark of a self-leader; yet so many people are oblivious to how they make decisions or are paralyzed by fear of the choices they face. This chapter explores both the confidence to make decisions and the process of making good decisions.

## YES OR NO?

When a surgeon makes an incision, he or she cuts into the body; when we make a decision, we cut through the choice of yes or no.

Decisions can be simple; for example: Will I have carrots or ice cream for a snack? In this choice we decide between the immediate taste sensation and the longer-term benefits to our health (especially our waistline!). Decisions can be complex when each of our options has both benefits and risks and we cannot know all the consequences of the decision. An example of a complex decision would be for an executive who must decide between three choices: (1) profit may increase by 20 percent but 10 percent of staff must be laid off, (2) profit may increase to 30 percent but 15 percent of staff will definitely be laid off, or (3) there will be no layoffs but profitability could go up or down.

There are three main reasons that people are prevented from making a decision: (1) they fear getting it wrong; (2) they don't think they have permission to say no, particularly to authority figures; (3) they don't think they have the right to say yes to what is important to them. Our ability to make yes and no choices is strongly impacted by our upbringing. If your caregivers were stern and said or inferred that your opinion didn't count or that you would be punished, then it is not surprising that making decisions would be difficult for you.

Table 4.1 is a quick assessment of your ability to say no to things.

We initially learn to make decisions from observing and imitating our parents or caregivers and, later on, by observing people around us (Bandura 1977). It's natural, though, that when we need to make decisions, we take into consideration the reactions of those around us. We usually don't want to disappoint those people with whom we identify, with whom we solidify and test our identity, and with whom we belong. Disregarding this group when we make our decisions could mean social rejection, something that for humans is equivalent to risking survival.

**TABLE 4.1**   Ability to Say No to Things

|  | Never | Sometimes | Always |
|---|---|---|---|
| Polite requests from your children | | | |
| An offer of food | | | |
| An offer of a drink | | | |
| A request to help | | | |
| A habit that you know is bad for you | | | |
| A request from your boss that you think doesn't make sense | | | |

## KNOWING WHAT YOU NEED

It has been proposed in Maslow's hierarchy of needs pyramid (Maslow 1943) that we operate from the most basic, primitive instincts, such as those related to having food and shelter, to the ultimate, more subtle needs of seeking spiritual evolution and connection. It appears that we are programmed to make decisions related to reproduction (i.e., the species' maintenance), self-protection, and status maintenance (Kenrick et al. 2010). Neuroscience research highlights the impact that ostracism and social rejection has on humans: Nobody likes to be left out. First, signals of rejection and ostracism can cause us physical pain; the continuation of the rejection will cause sadness and anger, evolving toward significant increases in blood pressure and stress hormones (in addition to higher self-reported levels of tension); we end up in a state in which brain activity is compromised and we cannot perform our work or personal duties well (Williams 2007). Without self-leadership, the work/home boundary can be breached by stress, risking career or marital harmony.

So with our biological and social programming, how do we become authentic and make conscious decisions that move us in the direction of our intentions? When we are in the process of making decisions, there are usually several aspects of our lives and survival at stake. We therefore need to be clear about the role these factors are playing within us, so that we can focus on our own effort to get where we want or need to be.

Just as the authors were writing this chapter, coauthor Andrew was coaching a businesswoman who had said yes to organizing a charity event even though she didn't want to. Andrew asked her if she could say no. Her response was, "I could, but I can't." This woman was not in control of her decision most likely because of an existing belief; perhaps she believed that others were more important than she was or that no one should say no to a good cause. Updating belief systems will be examined in Chapter 8.

To make good decisions we must have the will to make choices and a framework to evaluate them. In addition to will and a decision framework it is also helpful to have the time to reflect and consider our decisions, and with the fast pace of life and business today, that can be a challenge.

## REALITY IS ONLY REAL TO YOU

Before any of us can make effective decisions, we need to understand how we "map" reality. Much as we would like to believe that we are rational and objective, it appears that that is not the case.

For example, imagine you were trying to navigate across Paris but all you had was a map of London; no matter what decision you made, you would find it almost impossible to reach your destination. We navigate life using multiple mental maps that are constructed from our past experiences, assumptions, and conclusions.

Because the information used to make these maps was filtered by our values and beliefs, they are not always accurate.

Figure 4.1 illustrates the thinking process that we (rapidly) go through, usually without realizing it, to get from data (external reality) to a decision or action:

1. Observable "data" that we receive through our five senses about the world enters our "mental map."

2. We select which data or facts to pay attention to based on our beliefs and values from prior experience.

3. We apply our existing assumptions or conclusions, often without considering them.

4. We make personal and cultural meaning from these assumptions.

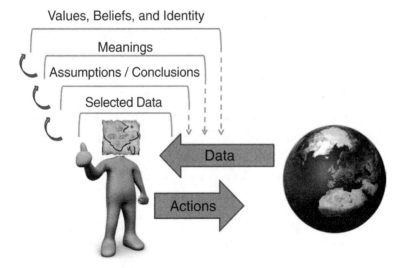

**FIGURE 4.1**  Understanding Mental Maps.

5. We develop or reinforce values and beliefs based on these conclusions.

6. We create a frame of mind about a person or situation.

7. We take action based on what we perceive as "right" based on our frame of mind.

Seems complicated? Consider the following example.

Oliver, now a lawyer in a large international firm, was told as a young boy that he was bright. However, at 11 years old he failed an exam to allow him to enter an elite school. His parents paid for him to go to another school where he worked very hard to gain entrance to a prestigious university.

Oliver concluded that working hard was the key to success. At the law firm as an adult, he assumed that if he just worked hard he would be promoted to partner. When other lawyers spent time going out to lunches and networking he discounted this behavior as "worthless," choosing to do what he thought was right. So when a less hard-working peer was promoted ahead of him he felt betrayed. Oliver was unaware of the cultural meanings at his law firm where networking and lunches were important actions in gaining partnership status. Only after he was passed over did he begin to notice the behaviors that were valued by the firm.

Can you see how Oliver made a frame of mind and made decisions based on this? He should have checked the facts before making important decisions. We all need to do that.

If Oliver had stopped for a moment, he could have asked himself:

- "Do I have all the information I need to be successful?"

- "What is my frame of mind?"

- "What are the rules of the game?"

In his book *Games Business Experts Play*, L. Michael Hall describes how frames of mind become the rules of the game. In Oliver's case, the authors are not saying that hard work doesn't equal success, but we are highlighting that Oliver was not aware of his frames of mind or the rules of the game at his law firm.

Typically, people make decisions with incomplete information and unconscious bias. With self-leadership we can all train ourselves to make better decisions and choose which games we want to play. In addition, this step-by-step reasoning process helps us remain objective and, when working or challenging others, reach a shared conclusion without conflict. We need to ask ourselves:

1. "Do I have all the facts?"

2. "Am I weighting the evidence equally or cherry-picking the facts that I like?"

3. "What do these facts mean? Could they mean something else? Am I considering the facts in the right context?"

4. "What am I assuming? What if this assumption wasn't true?"

5. "What conclusions am I making?"

6. "What do I believe? Am I being prejudiced or biased?"

7. "What is the correct action to take?"

This practice of observing decision making will reduce bad decisions and increase innovation and creativity. As you practice this skill you will gain greater confidence in your decision making and ability to make powerful choices. In addition, this step-by-step reasoning process helps you remain objective when working with or challenging others to reach a shared conclusion without conflict.

## MAJOR CHOICES

Life presents us with a large number of choices, including:

- Shall I work hard and get good grades, or should I goof off and have fun?

- What subjects should I study?

- Am I a good person?

- Shall I commit to this relationship?

- Should I take this job?

- Should I leave this job?

- Will I be happy?

As self-leaders we ask, "Did I make my life choices myself, or were they made for me?" and, "Did I consciously and intentionally make choices, or did I just drift with the tide?"

The good news is that the past does not equal the future and we can make new choices and rewrite beliefs about ourselves that don't serve us anymore.

Before you end this chapter, please consider an upcoming decision you need to make and run through the seven previous questions starting with, "Do I have all the facts?"

### Summary of the Chapter

Life and work are full of decisions that we must make every day. If we want to exercise the choices proposed on the last chapter, we need to familiarize ourselves with and master both the confidence to make decisions and the process of making good decisions. We also need to reprogram our past if that past taught us that we would be punished for our decisions or that our decisions wouldn't count. To make good decisions we must have the will to make choices and a framework to evaluate our choices. In addition to will and a decision framework, it is also helpful to have the time to reflect and consider our decisions. With the fast pace of life and business today, that can be a challenge. Typically, we make decisions with incomplete information and unconscious bias, as we see and understand the world within the bias of our own experiences, beliefs, and values. Our way to see the world is usually very unique to us and doesn't necessarily translate easily to others. We can train ourselves to understand the world from other people's perspective; then we can make better decisions by practicing self-observation in our decision making. As we practice this skill we gain greater confidence in our decision making and ability to make powerful choices. In addition, this step-by-step reasoning process helps us remain objective when working with or challenging others to reach a shared conclusion without conflict.

## CHAPTER 5

# Knowing What You Want

*Most men lead lives of quiet
desperation and go to the grave
with the song still in them.*
—HENRY DAVID THOREAU

The previous chapters explored how we can be the driver in our life and how we can make effective decisions; however, all this could be for naught if we don't know where we are going or what we want.

As a leadership consultant and coach, coauthor Andrew often encounters clients who have challenges defining what they want. Despite the difficulty defining what they *do* want, these clients can be very articulate about what they *don't* want: they don't want to be stressed, they don't want to worry about money, they don't want to be stuck in an unfulfilling job, they don't want to be sick, they don't want to be single, and they sometimes don't want to be married.

As a professor and a speaker, coauthor Ana notices that many people just go through life responding automatically, in a knee-jerk fashion, to all that it presents to them. They go through the phases almost unconsciously—without an aim and without any knowledge of what is really moving them, motivating them, and making them tick. Many of us live in the illusion that we can go through life without completely taking charge or taking responsibility for what we do, say, act, or think. People make the excuse that life or work can be so complex and unexpected that they just react to whatever happens to them or do what the boss tells them.

There is no assignment of blame here; people are not consciously being irresponsible. More often than not, such apparent disregard for our responsibility as human beings is a consequence of how we grew up. Depending on families we are born into, the communities in which we live, the schools we attend, the teachers we are assigned, the friends we meet, and the groups we gravitate toward, we may or may not be taught or be able to role-model essential life skills such as these:

- How to discover our blind spots

- How to think through things and make decisions

- How to be assertive without being aggressive

- How to select our friends and acquaintances

- How to respond to setbacks or crises

Without these skills, we can go through life "shooting from the hip"—following momentary passions and disregarding consequences for ourselves and others, making choices just because the options are easy to get, and letting chances to examine our inner self pass by.

This is like living in a fog, one of misunderstanding, incomprehension, and confusion and full of unseen rocks (i.e., problems) on which we can stumble once or many times. The purpose of this book is to clear the fog and invite you, regardless of your upbringing, to be responsible—to be a self-leader.

## FROM REACTIVE TO RESPONSIBLE

Unlike a new piece of consumer electronics, life does not come with a users' manual. Learning to live can be a haphazard process, which is why most people are driven by their need for survival and go about life just reacting to what happens to them. They do that while engaging in relationships that do not have clear boundaries and are not in alignment with their core values. Some people have a chance to study the human sciences, and thus they may learn the intricacies of human behavior. Others learn how to make informed behavioral decisions through coaching or therapy. Still others pick up snippets from self-help books and TV programs (such as *Oprah*). And some people accept, without question, what their religion tells them, while others actively search for a personal truth. The vast majority of them go through life sometimes stumbling, being pushed or pulled, without spending time for questioning or reflecting on how to live.

It is easy to live on automatic pilot. We have all been there at one time or another; we are studying, working, dating, and having families. The problem with the automatic mode is that it does not let us have a say in how our life goes. We choose things and we make many important decisions, but for the most part these decisions are in reaction to something that has happened or somebody that was in our life. They are not intentionally or authentically generated to fulfill something that we have individually and independently decided.

One of the symptoms of being in the automatic mode is that, deep inside, we live in discomfort—we don't feel happy or fulfilled with our lives. There is an overwhelming feeling inside of us that somehow we are failing. To have a say in our life means to plan it, to decide where and how we want to go, all based in a deep knowledge of who we are, what we want, and what makes us happy.

As the authors were writing this chapter, Steve Jobs passed away. Jobs, the founder and head of Apple, was a self-leader who was fully aware of his strengths and unapologetically used them to pursue his vision. He was often compared to a modern-day Thomas Edison, and we think you could also compare him to Galileo who similarly challenged authority and gave us a new way of looking at science rather than hanging on to outdated models. Jobs gave a commencement speech at Stanford University on June 12, 2005, in which he shared how he dropped out of college because "I had no idea what I wanted to do with my life and no idea how college was going to help me." After dropping out of school, Jobs then began to drop *in* to classes that interested him, explaining, "You've got to find what you love. And that is as true for your work as it is for your lovers. Your work is going to fill a large part of your life and the only way to be truly satisfied is to do what you believe is great work, and the only way to do great work is to love what you do."

Jobs had the opportunity at an early age of exploring the classes and the world to find what he really liked; he did it in such a way that he could harvest the fruits of an awesome attitude and pursue a very successful life. Many of us, however, have not had that chance when we were younger. Perhaps we lived in financial circumstances that impeded such exploration, or maybe the place where we lived didn't have good resources, good colleges, and good examples to guide us. We could use our circumstances as an excuse for not living our own lives, except that there are plenty of examples of people who have lived with self-leadership despite their circumstances. Timothy Ferriss in his book *The 4-Hour Workweek* shares many examples of how people will make excuses to do something even mildly challenging that would move them closer to the lives they dream of living. His book also contains some good case studies of people who have overcome the excuses, taken action, and achieved their goals.

Be warned: if you want to hang on to your excuses and remain a pawn in the game of life, stop reading now.

## RESPONSIBLE *FOR SELF* AND
## RESPONSIBLE *TO* AGREEMENTS

When you are living in automatic mode, you are just a passenger, but with self-leadership you are the driver of your life. You are responsible for your life because you are able to respond or, as we like to say, " response-able." You can choose your responses to any situation when you know where you are going and why you want to get there. Before exploring your own direction, you should be familiar with the difference between the things you are responsible *for* and those you are responsible *to*.

When we sign a check we are agreeing to pay a sum of money, and when we join a company we agree to give our time and energy to meet the organization's goals. In both these cases it is obvious what we are responsible *to*. But what about when two people get married and agree to behave a certain way? Or what about the situation in which your employees are not performing and your boss wants you to hit a target? In these two situations there is a clear responsibility *to* something but there is also a danger that we will feel responsible *for* someone (see Figure 5.1).

We are responsible *to* the commitments we make and to act according to formal and mutually understood promises and contracts; we are responsible *for* our own thoughts, feelings, speech, and behaviors. We can feel or be made to feel responsible for others' feelings and actions, but that is not healthy, as it allows those people to avoid using their own self-leadership. When we are responsible for ourselves, we can control our actions and reactions to what happens to us. If we try to be responsible for other people, we set ourselves up for unhappiness and failure because it is not possible to have total control over other people's thoughts, feelings, and actions.

# Responsible "To"

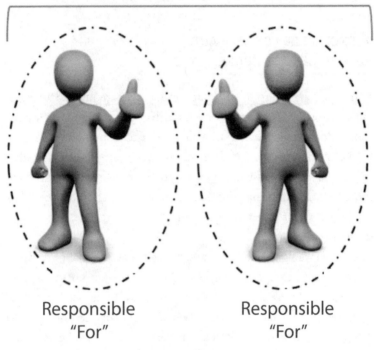

Responsible
"For"

Responsible
"For"

**FIGURE 5.1** Responsible *To* Versus Responsible *For*.

Without clarity, we can live our lives being either underresponsible or overresponsible. We are underresponsible if we don't take responsibility for our thoughts, feelings, speech, and behavior. We are underresponsible when we allow other people or circumstances to dictate how we live. We are overresponsible when we don't allow others to think and act for themselves or expect others to think, feel, speak, and behave in ways that make us happy.

Overresponsibility is strongly driven by culture. If, for example, coauthor Andrew asks a group in Asia, "Is a man responsible for his wife?" or, "Is a manager responsible for his subordinates?," he gets a resounding, "Yes!" If coauthor Ana asks the same question in

Brazil, she will get a positive answer as well. But if she were to ask this question in cultures with stronger individualism, such as in the United States, which encourages personal attainment and independence, the answer would be the opposite (Niedenthal, Krauth-Gruber, and Ric 2006). For a more comprehensive look at culture, see Chapter 9.

From a self-leadership perspective, a person is responsible to his partner, and a manager is responsible to his employees, just as he or she is responsible to the mission, vision, and goals of the company. Each person is responsible *for* himself or herself and *to* other individuals or groups in terms of the agreements made.

When we choose to be responsible to someone or something, we have entered into a contract, not necessarily a written one, and one that is not always articulated. For instance, if you join a sports team or a work team, you are contracting to play by the rules of the team as well as the rules of the game. You are responsible for your behavior but not for the behavior of the other players. Of course, in life these boundaries get blurred, people will try to make you responsible for them, and you may try to make them responsible for you. Clarity around our self-responsibility and our relationships helps us see through the fog and insulates us from being manipulated by others' agendas.

Instead of demanding that others talk or behave in a way that makes us happy, we can choose to lead ourselves and, if necessary, influence those people to behave differently. For example, if a teammate does not behave in a way that you feel is appropriate, you might be compelled to let him know that he is responsible for you feeling upset. This would likely lead to either defensiveness or aggressiveness from him. Alternatively, you could own your emotions and say something like, "When $X$ happens, I feel $Y$ emotion." Or you could bring his awareness to what you are both responsible to as team members and work together to achieve it. We will explore more examples of assertive communication in Chapter 6.

## LIVING ON PURPOSE

Self-leadership comes from a healthy balance of our focus on self and our focus on our relationships with others. Understanding the boundaries for our responsibility for and to others creates a foundation for us to be intentional, to live a life of purpose.

Figure 5.2 illustrates how our intention balances the many others in our life with our own purpose.

Remember the last time you flew on a plane? The door closes and locks and the stewards or stewardesses try, often in vain, to get us to listen to instructions of what happens should the air pressure in the plane drop. Their message is clear: "Help yourself to the oxygen mask *before* helping others." The rationale here is obvious: You can't help others if you are not thinking clearly.

Your relationship with others is best served by living your life authentically and on purpose. If you are responsible for yourself and respect what you need to be responsible to, this is not selfish; rather, you are being a role model that will inspire others.

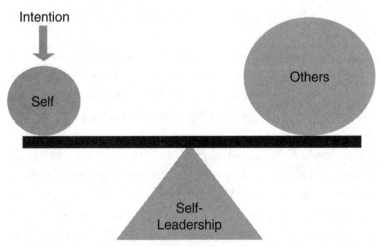

**FIGURE 5.2** Balancing Others in Our Life with Purpose and Intention.

It is amazing how much we can go through life worrying about what other people think about us or feeling responsible for them while ignoring what is important to us and living authentically.

Consider Figure 5.3. We do not live in isolation; we have many relationships. Ask yourself:

- "Am I being authentic in all areas of my life?"

- "Am I clear about what I am responsible for and to?"

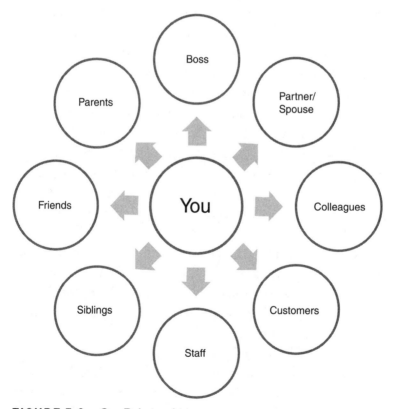

**FIGURE 5.3** Our Relationships.

- "Do I know what I want?"

- "Do I know what the other people in my life want?"

*Living and working with a purpose* means being knowledgeable, mindful, accountable, and responsible for each and every action we take, knowing that these actions will both reflect and define who we are, where we are going, and even the chances that we will really get there.

Living with a purpose means to really "connect the dots" of our life, to put our actions where our thoughts are; to align our thoughts with our dreams and our objectives; and to be fully conscious 24 hours a day, 7 days a week, as every little action we do carries with it intended and unintended consequences. If at least we are mindful of our actions, we have a good chance that all the consequences we get will be somewhat expected and accounted for.

Living with purpose does not necessarily mean that we must all discover a big transcendent reason for our existence (see Chapter 10). It can be as simple as waking up in the morning and knowing that we will choose to be in the now and do our best work. For many people, just knowing that today is a chance to learn and to grow as a person is intention enough; others prefer to be working toward a specific goal. Life goals should be more about being than about having.

It is understandable that we would all love to look attractive, feel powerful, and be fit, confident, and successful. Worldwide, success is recognized as involving looking and feeling good, having enough money to not have to worry about it, owning your own home, having a beautiful and healthy family, being recognized professionally, and helping others.

We have come to define success with having things; so, one of our most common thoughts is, "I need to have enough money in order to help my family, then I will be happy." Analyzing the last phrase gives us: "I need *to have* something, in order *to do* something else, so I can *be* something." The order of the thoughts expressed is: *to have—to do—to be.* The authors propose that instead we need *to be* someone who *does* things in order *to have* some other things: *to be— to do—to have.* We are human beings first and human doings second.

Tim Ferriss talks about dreamlining (the process of creating an imaginary timeline of what you want to be) and asks the question, "What would you do if there were no way that you could fail? If you were 10 times smarter than the rest of the world?" He encourages us to consider what we want to be, such as successful, and then asks what actions we would need to take to get there.

When coauthor Andrew decided it was time to look for a life partner, he listed the qualities that such a partner should have. After reviewing the list, he quickly realized that no woman with these qualities would be interested in the kind of man he was at that time. He immediately began to reflect on who he needed to be, and from this he began to behave differently; within six months he had the relationship he was looking for.

When coaching executives for their next level of promotion, coauthor Andrew has found that they get stuck in doing what they know how to do. But to be ready for the next step they really need to be leaders. When these executives begin to be and see themselves as leader, their actions change; shortly afterward, so do their actions.

If you are conflicted or don't know your intentions, your actions will not be authentic, and your results will be unlikely to give you satisfaction. This truth is often overlooked in business. A massive emphasis is placed on actions and results with little or no consideration as to whether employees know why they are being asked to do what they are doing. Kouzes and Posner touched on this topic with their concept of "encouraging the heart" in their 2002 book *The Leadership Challenge.* We will further explore this concept in Chapter 7 when we look at intrinsic motivation.

The book *Your Money or Your Life*, by Vicki Robin and Joe Dominguez (1999), has an interesting take on how the "having" can be unfulfilling, becoming more of a trap than a reward. Since the Industrial Revolution, most of us have learned to think that having material possessions is a good thing. We have been taught to always push for a higher standard of living as a path to happiness. Yet, what we find at the beginning of the twenty-first century is not only an economic crisis but a moral one as well, which has its roots in our own unbridled greed, among other things.

Instead of earning a living to really live a life, many people feel that their relationship with money has changed into one of worry and even despair. For those of us who have jobs—actually overworking to compensate for all the recent downsizing—by the time we account for going to and back from work, dressing for work, decompressing from work, and preparing our domestic routines to function while we are at work, we do very little that can be called living. We become our jobs and our work. For example, we, the authors, are no longer Ana and Andrew; we *are* a professor and a consultant.

Robin and Dominguez demonstrated the trap that we risk falling into if we consider *having things* as a synonym for happiness. They demonstrated that spending money and purchasing things just makes us happy up to a certain point, then those things become a burden that costs us more energy to be maintained than the energy it generates.

Sonia Lyubomirsky (2007) states that only 10 percent of our happiness comes from our circumstances. Her research suggests we have a genetic happiness set point but that a significant proportion of our happiness is under our own control. Sonia explores a number of strategies for increasing happiness, and foremost among these is gratitude—gratitude for what we have, for our relationships, and for what we are doing.

With self-leadership, we decide what we want to do with our lives and how we are going to live from here on. We don't need to purchase anything else that is not needed. Instead, we can focus on cultivating the kind of fulfillment that money cannot buy. We can choose to make a difference in the world by being ethical or by helping others with whatever skills and abilities we have. We can opt to make a difference by serving others, serving the world, rather than trying in vain to "keep up with the Joneses."

Throughout this book, the point is made that self-leadership is not selfish; self-leadership is not being preached so that everyone can just feather his or her own nest. Instead, self-leadership is advocated so that, by being able to take care of ourselves critically and independently, we liberate the people whom we have made responsible to take care of us. We can then join forces with other self-leaders to help everyone else make the transition to a more committed, conscious, and sustainable way of living together in this world.

Coauthor Andrew remembers a time, many years ago, when he was not in a happy place. "I had lost a business, my house, my car, and an important relationship," he says. "I was waiting in the rain for a bus feeling less than happy. The bus arrived, and as I stepped on, the driver said, 'Isn't it a great day?' I was tempted to respond with a sarcastic comment but stopped myself as I noticed the other passengers smiling at me. As I took my seat, I felt a little better about life, and then I noticed that the driver greeted every passenger the same way. Some of the passengers were obviously regulars and knew the driver by name, and others, like me, were transformed by his warm and upbeat greeting. As we reached the city and people disembarked, I wondered how much these happier people would influence their places of work. It was only after I got off the bus that I realized that this bus driver had a purpose—to make people smile—and no doubt he felt better in the process."

In another bus story, when coauthor Ana began what she calls her "second life" in the United States, after suffering a major life breakdown in her native Brazil, she would notice disabled people taking buses in Columbus, Ohio, where she was living. There would be blind folks—almost completely paralyzed individuals on wheelchairs. Somehow, every morning, they were on bus stops, and somehow (to Ana's eyes) they were able to catch a bus and go to work. Observing their resilience and that they too found a way to live productive lives—despite circumstances unimaginable to the rest of us—Ana was inspired to also find ways to overcome her life-changing difficulties and make a new beginning herself.

This chapter will finish with another story about an unlikely change agent; let's call him Malcolm. Malcolm, a lawyer in an international firm, had worked extremely hard to make equity partner, had reached his goal, and was now financially secure. Before Malcolm made it to equity, he struggled with the way the firm did things and often felt that he was not fully accepted there. Now, however, he felt he was on "the other side of the curtain" and understood, if not always agreed with, the way things were done. With 10 years left of his professional career, Malcolm could now cruise and keep the status quo, but he discovered a purpose. Malcolm knew that the communication at the firm was terrible and most people were operating from an "eat what you kill" competitive mindset; this was detrimental to their health and to that of the firm. He realized, however, that he could do something, and he set about changing the firm, starting with himself. Malcolm is role-modeling good communication and working with people in the firm to foster collaboration. He is sitting down with people and sharing with them self-leadership principles and supporting them through change. He is taking on more pro bono work for causes he cares about. Something changed in Malcolm. For him it is now no longer about making money; it is about making a difference.

## Summary of the Chapter

You have been challenged to consider whether you or the people around you are living on automatic pilot, clouded by a fog generated by your upbringing and experiences.

After reading this chapter, you are now more aware of the difference between what it is to be responsible *for* and responsible *to* in your relationships. So you can now avoid being manipulated to think and feel anything you don't want to.

As stated in standard instructions for airplane emergency procedures, you understand that you must help yourself first and then help others. This does not mean you are selfish; it means that you are healthy and more able to positively impact those around you.

Our actions—and our lives—can and must become purposeful when we stop wasting time in things that don't matter and don't contribute to our own life or to the lives of others. It is worth considering that at the end of Steve Jobs's amazing life, he refused to see people that came to visit him if he didn't think they were relevant to spend the precious time he had left. We surmise that he wanted to use his last hours and efforts wisely to do what really mattered to him and with people who would carry on his legacy.

Whether we have a short or long time on the planet, we think it is important to live authentically and with purpose. Will we make mistakes? We certainly will, but we can refocus and carry on. Actor Kevin Costner said, "I'm happy about the things I've done. Not always happy about the results, but happy about the decisions, because I made them myself. And I think that's an important way to go through life."

## CHAPTER 6

# Confidence and Communication

> *Our doubts are traitors, and make us
> lose the good we oft might win by
> fearing to attempt.*
> —WILLIAM SHAKESPEARE,
> *Measure for Measure*, ACT I, SCENE 4

Two qualities that are correlated with success in today's world are confidence and the ability to communicate effectively. It is not surprising, therefore, that we feel that self-confidence and communication are fundamental to self-leadership. Confidence is a state of mind and body, and effective communication, both verbal and nonverbal, emanates from that confidence.

Confidence is a sense of certainty about something such as, "I am confident the sun will rise tomorrow." Self-confidence is a belief or certainty in oneself, and the self-confident person can say, "I count on myself. I do what I say."

This does not necessarily mean that we believe ourselves to be invincible or infallible. Instead, we remind ourselves, "I can handle this. I can overcome this challenge."

The "noninfallibility" here is an important distinction. It is co-author Ana's experience that many people shy away from embracing self-confidence because they feel that they cannot control all the outcomes of whatever they do, particularly those things that depend on other people. The important thing here is that action needs to be taken on one's commitments. Repeated instances of that behavior will add up in our minds, ending up instilling a sense of self-confidence that we can achieve what we set ourselves up to achieve. When we are our words (i.e., when we own what we say), we become self-confident because we build a track record from doing what we say that we will do.

Confidence also can be transferred, and this is known as the Pygmalion or Rosenthal effect. If you had a teacher or significant adult who believed in your potential and abilities, chances are that you flourished under the influence of this positive expectation and transfer of confidence. This is important to remember when we lead others; we must believe in them and have confidence in them if we want them to develop.

Some people seem to be born with an abundance of confidence, while others seem timid and fearful. With them, practicing self-leadership builds their confidence through action, resulting in more confident action. This creates a reinforcing loop from confidence to competence, with competence reinforcing confidence (see Figure 6.1).

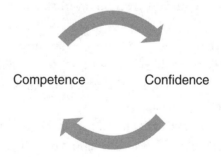

Competence          Confidence

**FIGURE 6.1**   A Reinforcing Loop.

Consider public speaking. It creates a level of anxiety in most people, with some absolutely terrified of the prospect of standing in front of an audience. To be effective as public speakers we must have self-confidence, and to do this requires facing the fear and taking action, which in turn build competence. The best public speakers have given thousands of speeches and have made many more mistakes than the novice.

Confidence is not a guarantee of success, but it puts us in the best state of mind and body to succeed. The famous basketball player Michael Jordan once said: "I have missed more than 9,000 shots in my career. I've lost almost 300 games. Twenty-six times I've been trusted to take the game's winning shot . . . and missed. I've failed over and over and over again in my life. And that is why I succeeded."

American inventor Thomas Alva Edison said about the difficulties he faced while trying to invent the lightbulb, that he had found 10,000 ways that it wouldn't work, but "every wrong attempt discarded is often a step forward" (Baldwin 2001).

Like everyone else, the self-confident individual faces uncertainty or fear but, while not knowing the outcome, takes action, confident in his or her ability to learn from feedback and to try again.

Healthy self-confidence is fueled by purpose (intention) and moderated by the ability to accept one's mistakes (fallibility). It is important to realize that failure is a function of time. If you have the time to take the feedback and make adjustments, any event is not a failure but a "learning experience," as Edison put it. Self-leaders, therefore, live by a mantra—"There is no failure, only feedback for improvement"—because they have the confidence that they can learn from mistakes and move forward.

Each success reinforces self-confidence, but early failures or the inability to adapt to feedback can lead many people to have low self-confidence. Remember the analogy with the deck of cards from Chapter 1. In life, some people are handed great cards in terms of opportunities, supportive parents, families, and/or communities, but others have all sorts of impediments to success. Perceived failures, or the repeated inability to reach desired results, can drain a person's strength and determination as well as the ability to feel confident. Unforgiving circumstances, repeated difficulties, or just bad luck can cause even the most confident individuals to doubt their abilities or feel the sting of insecurity.

Simply put, our brain learns based on what happens to us. If we repeatedly experience what may look like failure and exclusion from the desirable groups, our pain can indeed become physical. Some social psychology researchers are convinced that, for the brain, the pain caused by social exclusion equals the pain caused by physical discomforts such as hunger or injury (Eisenberger, Lieberman, and Williams 2003). When facing that kind of pain—social or other—our brain gets into the mode of "fight or flight." All the brain's abilities will be deviated from higher intelligence tasks to the protection mode.

Say someone faces a difficult environment at the office, such as not being trusted or being bullied by his or her coworkers. Even if he or she is ordinarily confident, the brain may fall into the fight-or-flight mode, making that person less able to solve problems or be creative.

When we are faced with such a situation, neurobiology comes to our rescue with the information that the brain is plastic in the sense that even after repeated failure, even after a learned lack of confidence, we can reestablish the neuronal connection of action–success–self-confidence through learning new behaviors (Eisenberger et al., 2003).

Conventional wisdom suggests that it is hard to change behavior. Although it is not easy, it *is* possible. Psychologist and education specialist Matthew Lieberman  studied how we learn in a way that changes our brain connections (Lieberman and Eisenberger 2009). When the environment is optimal, we can pay what he called "mindful attention" to what is being told or taught to us, and increase our ability to learn something new. According to Lieberman, we get into that *learning* state of mind when we feel protected and safe. Specifically, Lieberman mentioned the following factors as being conducive to a learning state and mindful attention:

- Status

- Certainty

- Autonomy

- Connection

- Justice

*Status* means the guarantee that we will not lose what we have achieved so far. *Certainty* means the ability to trust who is teaching, the thought that we will not be misled. *Autonomy* means the ability to make a choice, to decide whether or not we want to be there or to learn. It says that no one can be forced to learn and no one can impose *learning* on anybody else. Adults will only learn when they want to. The authors have both experienced this in our trainings and so give participants the power to choose when and what they learn.

*Connection* refers to having empathy from others, from peers, from superiors, and from who is teaching or transmitting anything new. It is the feeling of belonging somewhere, with a group, which makes us feel safe and confident in letting go of the distraction of other thoughts to focus solely on what is at hand to learn. Finally, the concept of *justice* reflects on fairness, knowing that we will not be misjudged, misrepresented, made a fool of, or sabotaged. It is the feeling that we will be given a fair chance to learn and perform at our best. When all of these criteria are met, our brain is free to pay mindful attention and learn new behaviors; thus, we can start to establish new neural connections and relearn self-confidence.

When we perform something successfully, our brain and our body retain the image, the movements, and the thought process that led to success. Success reinforces confidence, just as working out in the gym builds muscle. This analogy gives us the strategy for building self-confidence. When we go into the gym we do not pick up the heaviest weight there; instead, we pick one that is within our ability. When building your own self-confidence or coaching someone else to increase her or his confidence, start with an activity that is a stretch but also achievable.

Just as your mind and body learn from performing successful tasks, they can learn from imagination or visualization. Just by accessing the memory or imagination of confidence you can cue your body to be in a confident state before starting an activity, thus increasing your chances of success.

Coauthor Andrew has used the following exercise, learned from Dr. Bobby Bodenhamer and Dr. L. Michael Hall, to coach hundreds of people to perform better.

---

**Accessing and Amplifying Confidence**

1. Access a memory of something you are 100 percent confident you can do. It needs to be something that if someone asked, "Can you do this?" you would respond with a strong, "Of course!" It could be a task as simple as tying your shoelaces, brushing your teeth, or boiling an egg. Be aware of the feeling of this certainty in your body. Pay attention to how you breathe when you are 100 percent confident. Also notice your posture, your inner dialogue, and most importantly the way the world looks as you see it through the eyes of confidence.

2. Amplify this feeling of confidence. Imagine taking this feeling and doubling it. Visualize the You for whom confidence is no problem.

3. Anchor this feeling. Create a trigger for yourself so that you can remember this feeling. An anchor can be a gesture such as making a fist, a phrase you can say to yourself, or your favorite movie soundtrack (such as *Eye of the Tiger* from *Rocky*) playing in your head and lifting your confidence.

4. Apply this confidence to something you need to do with slowly increasing challenges. For instance, if you need to speak publicly, first apply the confidence in talking to one person, then to a small group of people you know, and finally to a large group of strangers in a formal speech.

Doing this exercise will help you create a foundation for self-confidence that you can build on with each successful action. Choose to access and amplify the feeling of confidence before any important interaction with other people (e.g., a phone call or meeting).

Some experts advise us to dress confidently and walk confidently to "fake it till you make it." These techniques will work for a time, but only if you have the foundation of self-confidence, and this foundation is not dependent on external factors. Confidence comes from your self-leadership over your thoughts, feelings, speech, and actions.

Self-confidence is not dependent on others. With self-confidence as part of your self-leadership you will not worry about what others think of you. Instead, you will focus on the adjustments you need to make to your communication or your behaviors to achieve your outcomes.

Psychologist Albert Bandura expanded on the concept of self-confidence when he wrote about self-efficacy. Self-efficacy is the belief that you are capable of performing in a certain manner to attain certain goals. For example, imagine you are dropped in a foreign city where you do not speak the language. Could you get to the train station, buy a ticket, and board a train to another city 500 miles away? If your answer is yes and you have never had to do this before, then you have self-efficacy, the confidence in your own abilities.

With self-leadership we use self-efficacy to turn ideas into actions and actions into results.

## FINDING YOUR VOICE

One of the consequences of self-leadership is that you develop a voice. Your voice is your authentic and assertive expression of your thoughts and feelings. Many people fail to develop their voice or lose their power to authentically express themselves for myriad reasons. Some people overcompensate for some deep-seated fear by using their voice in an overly loud or aggressive fashion.

So, how do you find your own voice? And what benefits to business and society accrue when you (and people like you) can speak with respect to yourself and to others?

Somewhat paradoxically, before any of us can speak authentically we must first learn to listen—listen to ourselves and listen to others. Listening is not the same as hearing. Hearing is an involuntary physical and biological act. There is no understanding or appropriate response. Listening is a conscious act. It involves hearing, receiving, comprehending, and responding appropriately. (The topic of listening is discussed at length in Chapter 7.)

Listening to others is about paying attention to what is important to those people and from there discovering what their needs are. As mentioned in Chapter 4, humans construct value and meaning, and this drives our behaviors. You can "listen" for other people's needs by observing what they invest time and energy in. Or when people are doing or talking about something that they are energized by or connected to, you can ask them, "What's important about that?" From their response you will begin to discover their values.

There are basically three ways we can communicate: aggressively, passively, or assertively (authentically). These are defined, in turn, as follows:

**Aggressive**: An expression of needs, wants, feelings, beliefs, or opinions without regard for what others want.

**Passive**: Not expressing, or downplaying, wants, feelings, beliefs, and opinions.

**Assertive** (authentic): An honest, direct, and confident expression of needs, wants, feelings, beliefs, or opinions that allows and actively encourages others to express themselves.

Aggressive communicators may be narcissistic, selfish, and/or autocratic. Perhaps they may have learned this behavior or it is a compensation for a fear of showing their vulnerability. Consider the outcomes of this type of behavior. Aggressiveness can reap short-term benefits, and as people comply through intimidation their response will only serve to reinforce the behavior. Aggressive communication will decrease the number and quality of the relationships that people have through life, and such people may be oblivious to the lack of autonomy they are creating around them. The cycle can continue when they become even more frustrated by the passive-aggressiveness of people fed up with being treated with disrespect.

Passive communicators usually believe that they are being polite and are confused by people not taking the time to understand what is important to them. In Asia there is a cultural norm to not speak up first and definitely not if there is a more senior person in the room; this stems from a belief that it is wrong to be "the sound of an empty vessel" because an empty vessel is noisy but has no content. The passive communicator dislikes overt conflict, which means that many issues are not addressed, and this leads to deep-seated resentment.

Interestingly Sun Tzu, author of the 2,500-year-old Chinese strategy book *The Art of War*, says, "If the situation offers victory but the ruler forbids fighting, the general may still fight. If the situation is such that he cannot win, then the general must not fight even if the ruler orders him to fight."

To a modern ear, this sounds very aggressive, in effect, saying, "Fight if you can win, and don't if you can't." But according to Sun Tzu expert Khoo Kheng-Hor, this translates into a modern context as, "Be a professional, don't be a 'yes' man, speak up, and do what is right." Of course, some diplomacy will be required if you disagree with a superior or you will be performing a CLM—career-limiting move!

Self-leaders express themselves authentically and assertively; they know what they want to say and why they want to say it. They understand that conflicting perspectives are normal but through communication these differences in opinion do not need to lead to conflict or aggressive behaviors. The self-leader's highest intent is for both parties to understand each other's beliefs and work collaboratively. They do this by "seeking first to understand and then to be understood," which is Habit Five of Stephen Covey's Seven Habits.

Our self-leadership habits for speaking up would be:

1. Position yourself as a trusted ally with the other person's best interest at heart.

2. Respect the other person's perspective, and acknowledge it.

3. Confidently but gently offer your thoughts as an alternate perspective to achieve a solution that is mutually beneficial.

4. To achieve point 2, use the other person's preferred communication style and, if possible, use an appropriate analogy that gets his or her attention.

5. Listen carefully to the other person challenge your idea and defend his or her own.

6. Restate the key points of your idea in a way that connects to the other person's outcomes.

7. Keep your ego in check, and share credit for the idea, if it is adopted.

Speaking up with authenticity requires that we have clear personal boundaries. Recall the discussion in Chapter 3 of the four powers of being human and in Chapter 5 of what it means to be responsible *for* and *to*. If we put these two concepts together, we can create the boundary between Me and Not Me.

Me is everything we are responsible for—our thoughts, feelings, speech, and behavior. Not Me is everybody else's stuff. Understanding and applying this truth is empowering and transformational, as the authors can attest from our own experience and the people we have worked with. (See Chapter 11 for how to coach this skill.)

Let's say you are having a disagreement with someone and she says or does something potentially cruel and hurtful. Typically, you will choose to respond aggressively or passively, telling her that she is wrong and escalating things by saying something equally cruel. Or you can take what she says to heart and feel your self-esteem crushed. With the Me–Not Me boundary in place you can stop the insult literally at arm's length and recognize that whatever the other person says or does is not you; it is just someone else's perception filtered through his or her mental maps (see Chapter 4). You do not need to make it your truth.

In addition to taking responsibility when receiving communication, we must be careful with our own language. Dr. Marshall B. Rosenberg, in his book *Nonviolent Communication*, gives the following examples.

1. The use of the phrase *have to*, as in, "There are some things you have to do, whether you like it or not," illustrates how personal responsibility for our actions can be obscured by speech.

   When we share this point we often meet with resistance. "But there are things I have to do!" we hear. Not true, there are things you have chosen to do because the consequences of not doing them are undesirable. People say things like, "I have to go to work," and we understand that they say this because they need money to support themselves and their families, but going to work is still a choice. If we choose not to work, the consequences could be dire but we could choose to get a different job or start a business. When we say, "We have to . . ." our physiology responds as if we are being forced and we are therefore unmotivated; however if we say, "I choose to go to work" our physiology responds as if we are in control and we feel energized and mobilized.

2. The phrase *makes one feel*, as in "You make me feel guilty," is another example of how language facilitates denial of personal responsibility of our own feelings and thoughts. Nobody *makes you feel an emotion; you choose to respond with that emotion to a real or imagined trigger.*

We are not exercising self-leadership when we attribute the cause of our actions to factors outside ourselves. The communication usually takes the form of "I did $Y$ behavior because of $X$ trigger"; for example:

"I was rude to my colleague because of the e-mail he sent me."

"I had to have a drink because it was a client function."

"I am angry because you didn't do what I asked."

"I had to eat all the food because otherwise it would have been a waste."

Nonviolent communication (NVC) offers us a process to step back and communicate authentically with an assertive and measured response, with the following process:

1.  **Observation.** We see or hear what is actually happening, what people are saying or doing that is impacting us, and avoid judgment or blame.

2.  **Feelings.** We state what we feel when we observe: Are we hurt, scared, joyful, amused, or irritated?

3.  **Needs.** We say what our needs are connected to the feelings we have identified.

4.  **Request.** We communicate, verbally or by other means, without demand, what we prefer would happen in the future.

The following examples should give you the idea so that you can start practicing this in your life, if you are not already.

- A coworker is making disparaging comments about your work, which you know to be of excellent quality.

  - You realize that your work is under your control (Me) and your coworker's comments are not in your control (Not Me).

  - You take ownership of your emotions so that you can respond with calmness and confidence.

  - You say something like, "When I hear comments like this (observation), I am disappointed (feeling) with the lack of team cooperation. I am open to constructive feedback (need), and in the future I would welcome (request) your observations to ensure the highest quality for our team.

- Your boss has made several decisions that negatively impact your workflow without consulting you.

  - Instead of just passively accepting this situation and harboring resentment you choose an appropriate time to discuss this with your boss, saying something like, "I think I understand your reasons for making changes; however, when changes are made without my input I feel disempowered. I believe I have some good observations and ideas from my experience, and in the future I respectfully request that you give me the opportunity to share these before a decision is made."

- You are having an argument with your spouse, and he accuses you of being selfish and thoughtless, among other things.

  - Rather than respond with a list of your spouse's faults, which is sure to make things worse, you take a step back and access your four powers.

- You calmly let your spouse know that you have heard his list of complaints.

- You apologize that he is perceiving things this way and let him know that you feel hurt that your intentions have been misunderstood. Then you tell him that in the future you would prefer to receive his feedback immediately so that issues can be addressed one by one rather than as a list of charges.

Your situations may be similar to or different from those above. Yet hopefully you can feel the freedom of not being responsible for others' thoughts and feelings about you. By not reacting to their mental map, you have the chance to show them who you authentically are and to protect your self-esteem. Maybe they will change their opinion and actions, and maybe they won't, but you won't be held emotionally hostage by the situation; you can focus on building relationships and engaging in tasks that really matter.

As an exercise, consider a situation where you need to speak authentically. Then write a script using the framework described here. Practice saying this script while accessing your state of confidence. When the appropriate time arises, use your "voice" in an assertive and authentic way.

Developing our communication skills, whether through listening, speaking, or asking questions, is perhaps the single most important skill we can develop to improve the quality of our lives. The challenge is just the sheer volume of communication we are now exposed to. There is our own internal dialogue as well as requests from family members, colleagues, clients, officials, and so on. We are all experiencing data overload and attention deficit (see Figure 6.2).

Being aware of this "information storm," we can be empathetic when communicating with other people who are experiencing the same distractions. Don't fall into the trap of assuming that when

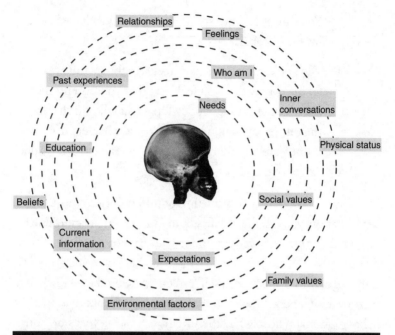

**FIGURE 6.2** Layers of Thoughts.

others don't understand us they are bad listeners, yet when we do not understand them we attribute this to their being bad communicators.

The key to effective communication is to get the listeners' attention first (Berlo 2003). We must connect to what is of interest or value to them and be prepared to repeat the message to get noticed above all the competing information.

Research with 60 executives over a one-week period (Davenport and Beck 2000) showed that these are the factors most highly associated with getting attention:

1. The message is personalized.

2. It evokes an emotional response.

3. It comes from a trustworthy source or respected sender.

4. It is concise.

Communication scientists say that you need to be flexible with different ways of getting attention and getting your message across if you want to guarantee you will be heard.

To be effective in communication, self-leaders need not only to work on their assertiveness but also to convey confidence and trust so that people can want to listen to them. Then, responsibly, self-leaders need to choose to understand the communication context and work with it.

## Summary of the Chapter

Self-confidence is about counting on ourselves, knowing that we will do what we say we will do. Confidence can be learned, built, and rebuilt, if necessary. When we have confidence in our actions, we develop competence. Confidence is also about finding our own voice and using it. Finding our voice doesn't mean speaking up aggressively or loudly; instead, it means speaking up with confidence. We can have a voice and have the confidence to use it. Communicating aggressively or passively does not pay off over time. Being assertive—the best way to communicate—is being authentic about what we think and what we feel in a way that respects others. We can establish our Me–Not Me boundary to protect our self-esteem and to help us create our communication in a way that doesn't escalate conflict; instead, it makes us effective in relating to others.

## CHAPTER 7

# Personality, Strengths, and Motivation

> *Always be yourself, express yourself, have faith in yourself; do not go out and look for a successful personality and duplicate it.*
>
> —BRUCE LEE

A definition of self-leadership that the authors have often used is:

Self-leadership is having a developed sense of who you are, what you can do, and where you are going coupled with the ability to influence your communication, emotions, and behavior on the way to getting there.

Let's break this down to fully understand it. If you were to be asked, "Who is Jennifer Lopez?" you would likely respond, "A singer or a judge of *American Idol*." If you were to be asked, "Who is Leonardo DiCaprio?" you would likely answer, "An actor." It is interesting that when we are asked *who* someone is we answer with *what* they do.

Self-leadership requires that you consider *who* you are as being separate from *what* you do and how you do it. This raises the existential and philosophical question: "Who am I?"

Cynics might say that for an individual to talk about, explain, understand, or judge oneself is linguistically impossible, since it requires the self to understand itself. According to Swiss psychologist Jean Piaget, consciousness is infinitely "reflexive." This means that we have the ability to endlessly think about our thinking, feel about our feelings, think about our feelings, about our thoughts or imaginations, or any combination of these.

The important thing is to recognize that self is not a fixed object but a fluid process. We have the ability to simultaneously be self and at the same time, step back and observe ourselves and choose to change (see Chapter 4).

> *We are not nouns, we are verbs. I am not a thing—an actor, a writer—I am a person who does things—I write, I act—and I never know what I am going to do next. I think you can be imprisoned if you think of yourself as a noun.*
> —STEPHEN FRY

## PERSONALITY

We often talk about ourselves and others in terms of personality. The word *personality* comes from the Latin *persona*, which refers to the masks worn by actors in ancient times. Today the term *personality* refers to the set of predictable behaviors by which we profile a person. These are known as "traits."

Many discussions have taken place as to whether traits really exist, and there is a clear danger of falling into the trap of "labeling" yourself or others based on a few behaviors observed in only one context. This is what we call "putting people in a box."

Albert Einstein once said: "Everybody is a genius. But if you judge a fish by its ability to climb a tree, it will live its whole life believing that it is stupid." And this is exactly what happens to many of us as we are judged by attributes that we don't necessarily have and live our lives believing that we are stupid when actually we are not exercising the best of our potentialities. This is why it is important to find out what "makes you tick" and how to use your strengths.

The ancient Greek physician Hippocrates recorded the first known personality model, postulating that someone's persona is based upon four separate temperaments: air, water, earth, and fire. Another Greek physician extended Hippocrates' theory by applying a body fluid to each temperament: blood, mucus, black bile, and yellow bile, respectively. The fluid that was dominant was said to be the person's "humor."

Since that time, thinking about personality in four boxes created along two axes has become an unconscious paradigm for most Western thinkers. Carl Gustav Jung (1875–1961), the founder of analytical psychology, categorized mental functioning along the axes of sensing/intuition and thinking/feeling. See Table 7.1 for descriptions of these concepts.

The Myers-Briggs Type Indicator (MBTI), developed during World War II, is a personality type assessment that expanded on Carl Jung's psychological types. The MBTI test uncovers your preferences within four dichotomies, as shown in Table 7.1.

For coauthor Ana, the MBTI brought peace about who she was and helped her find her "tribe"—other people just like her. Using MBTI or any of the myriad personality models may help us find out a lot about ourselves and what we have in common with others. For instance, if you are an introvert and have a sensing preference, you can see the introvert in someone else, even if he or she does not have a sensing preference. This does help us see that we

**TABLE 7.1**   The Four Myers-Briggs Type Indicator Dichotomies

| EXTRAVERSION | INTROVERSION |
|---|---|
| A preference for directing energy outward, to other people and objects | Preference for focusing thoughts and energy on inner experiences, thoughts, and ideas, rather than in outer events |
| **SENSING** | **INTUITION** |
| Preference to consider only what can be perceived by the five senses: touch, smell, sight, taste, hearing | Inclination to consider proprietarily what one's intuition tells/signals than factual information |
| **THINKING** | **FEELING** |
| A preference for making decisions with objectivity and detachment, logically and as far as possible from feelings | Preference for deciding based on personal and social values, seeking harmony and understanding |
| **JUDGING** | **PERCEIVING** |
| Being decisive, seeking closure and results to projects and problems, whether through thinking or feeling | Flexibility and spontaneity toward finishing projects, reaching conclusions, dealing with the world, preferably using Sensing or Intuition modes (sensing or intuition) |

Based on *MBTI Manual*, 1998.

have something in common with almost anyone, and it can help increase our tolerance of others . . . and of ourselves.

In the mid-1970s Richard Bandler and Leslie Cameron-Bandler took another approach to describing personality with the concept of meta-programs. Meta-programs occur because we respond not to reality but to our internal mental map of reality.

We receive information from the world and filter that information through our language and neurology; we then make meaning from this information and evaluate and frame it using cognition (see Figure 7.1). The result is a "frame of mind" that acts as a filter for any new information received and governs our thinking, feeling, and behaviors. This frame-of-mind filter is named "meta-program" because it is meta (above representation) and repeats itself (a program).

Drs. L. Michael Hall and Bobby G. Bodenhamer expanded on the work of Bandler and others in their book *Figuring out People* (1997/2000). They explained that meta-programs arise from both nature and nurture. These "frames of mind" influence our eyes, ears, and bodies and becomes the way we perceive and behave in the world.

Meta-programs operate on a continuum: if you are not at either extreme of the continuum, a particular factor will not be an

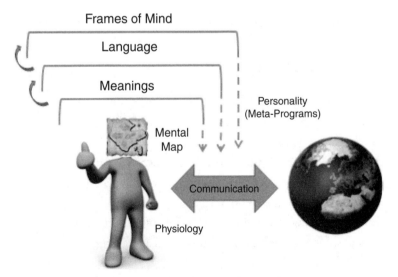

**FIGURE 7.1** Frames of Mind Creating Personality

obvious part of your personality, but if your default way of being is skewed to one end or another, this will be a "driver" of your way of being. When you can easily move back and forth along the continuum you will have more choices and power in different contexts.

Over 50 meta-programs have been catalogued, including the four dimensions of the MBTI. Here are four important ones for you to consider to better get to know yourself and others.

## Chunk Size

Do you prefer to just get the "big picture" about something, or are you more interested in the details?

People who prefer the big chunks of information can find details boring and a barrier to getting things done, and people who value details can evaluate big-picture information as fluff, having no substance.

Where are you? Detail-------------Both-------------Big picture

## Matching/Mismatching

Most people prefer to look for similarities. They either like to match new information with what they already know or will try to match pieces of data to each other. But some people look for differences; they mismatch any new data as part of their process of understanding it. You can identify people with a mismatching meta-program by the fact that they say, "yes but . . ." whenever presented with new information. If you have flexibility, you can move back and forth between matching and mismatching.

Where are you? Matching--------------Both------------- Mismatching

## Relationship to Time

Some people experience time as if there is an eternal "now." They lose track of time, are spontaneous, and focus on the current experience, which can cause them to be late to scheduled events. We call these people "In Time" because they easily get lost in time.

Other people experience time as if it exists outside of their body. They process time as if it moves alongside them. These "Through Time" people are more sequential, linear, and "on time."

**Where are you? In time (spontaneous)-------Through time (scheduled)**

## Reference to Self or Other

We can choose to think and behave solely based on our own view of the world; we can choose to think and behave in reference to what others deem "right"; or we can have a balance between both.

Self-referent people can be oblivious to others' needs or wants. They make assumptions based primarily on their own internal thinking and feelings and usually discount information that others offer; they do not notice other people's physiology and miss many nonverbal clues. Because of this, they will have difficulty establishing rapport.

"Other" referent people pay attention to others' needs and wants. They are willing to enter other people's models of the world and to accept or validate them. Taken to the extreme these people will put others' needs and wants ahead of their own, causing a loss of autonomy.

**Where are you? Self------------Both----------------Other**

We have described two models for assessing and describing personality, but there are many more. For example, Paul T. Costa and Robert R. McCrae did a large-scale analysis of all the observable types and traits and created a "Big Five" Personality Test, which has been scientifically validated and is useful for hiring and developing individuals and teams. We are not promoting any one type of assessment, only suggesting that you should explore your personality using the tools that are available to you, because self-awareness gives us choice.

## VALUES

Chapter 5 discussed being authentic and finding our intention. We are authentic and intentional when we are living based on our core values. Values are personal or shared enduring beliefs or ideals about what is good or desirable and what is not. Personal values evolve from circumstances in our lives and can change over time. Values are considered to be subjective and vary across people and cultures.

Values operate as a high-level "frame of mind" or intention and thus influence all other aspects of our personality. Knowing what we value and believe in is a large step toward knowing who we are.

What we value is often unconscious or out of our awareness. Can you name at least three values that guide any and all of your behaviors?

Table 7.2 is a list of values for you to consider. As you examine your values, think more in final terms—that is, which ones you absolutely cannot live without, the deal breakers, the ones that if you don't see them in the people with whom you associate, you cannot stay close to them.

*These* are your core values!

As you review the list in Table 7.2, check off all values that apply to you. Now, from all the values chosen, select your top seven values. Use Table 7.3 for your work. Here's a hint to help you

**TABLE 7.2** Core Values

| | | |
|---|---|---|
| – Abundance | – Balance | – Consistency |
| – Acceptance | – Beauty | – Contentment |
| – Accessibility | – Being the best | – Continuity |
| – Accomplishment | – Belonging | – Contribution |
| – Accuracy | – Benevolence | – Control |
| – Achievement | – Bliss | – Conviction |
| – Acknowledgment | – Boldness | – Conviviality |
| – Activeness | – Bravery | – Coolness |
| – Adaptability | – Brilliance | – Cooperation |
| – Adoration | – Buoyancy | – Cordiality |
| – Adroitness | – Calmness | – Correctness |
| – Adventure | – Camaraderie | – Courage |
| – Affection | – Candor | – Courtesy |
| – Affluence | – Capability | – Charity |
| – Aggressiveness | – Care | – Charm |
| – Agility | – Carefulness | – Chastity |
| – Alertness | – Celebrity | – Cheerfulness |
| – Altruism | – Certainty | – Clarity |
| – Ambition | – Challenge | – Cleanliness |
| – Amusement | – Cleverness | – Clear-mindedness |
| – Anticipation | – Closeness | – Craftiness |
| – Appreciation | – Comfort | – Creativity |
| – Approachability | – Commitment | – Credibility |
| – Articulacy | – Compassion | – Cunning |
| – Assertiveness | – Completion | – Curiosity |
| – Assurance | – Composure | – Daring |
| – Attentiveness | – Concentration | – Decisiveness |
| – Attractiveness | – Confidence | – Decorum |
| – Audacity | – Conformity | – Deference |
| – Availability | – Congruency | – Delight |
| – Awareness | – Connection | – Dependability |
| – Awe | – Consciousness | – Depth |

(continued)

**TABLE 7.2** Core Values (Continued)

| | | |
|---|---|---|
| – Desire | – Excellence | – Friendliness |
| – Determination | – Excitement | – Frugality |
| – Devotion | – Exhilaration | – Fun |
| – Devoutness | – Expectancy | – Gallantry |
| – Dexterity | – Expediency | – Generosity |
| – Dignity | – Experience | – Gentility |
| – Diligence | – Expertise | – Giving |
| – Direction | – Exploration | – Grace |
| – Directness | – Expressiveness | – Gratitude |
| – Discipline | – Extravagance | – Gregariousness |
| – Discovery | – Extroversion | – Growth |
| – Discretion | – Exuberance | – Guidance |
| – Diversity | – Fairness | – Happiness |
| – Dominance | – Faith | – Harmony |
| – Dreaming | – Fame | – Health |
| – Drive | – Family | – Heart |
| – Duty | – Fascination | – Helpfulness |
| – Dynamism | – Fashion | – Heroism |
| – Eagerness | – Fearlessness | – Holiness |
| – Economy | – Ferocity | – Honesty |
| – Ecstasy | – Fidelity | – Honor |
| – Education | – Fierceness | – Hopefulness |
| – Effectiveness | – Financial | – Hospitality |
| – Efficiency | independence | – Humility |
| – Elation | – Firmness | – Humor |
| – Elegance | – Fitness | – Hygiene |
| – Empathy | – Flexibility | – Imagination |
| – Encouragement | – Flow | – Impact |
| – Endurance | – Fluency | – Impartiality |
| – Energy | – Focus | – Independence |
| – Enjoyment | – Fortitude | – Industry |
| – Entertainment | – Frankness | – Ingenuity |
| – Enthusiasm | – Freedom | – Inquisitiveness |

**TABLE 7.2**  Core Values (Continued)

| | | |
|---|---|---|
| – Insightfulness | – Mellowness | – Popularity |
| – Inspiration | – Meticulousness | – Potency |
| – Integrity | – Mindfulness | – Power |
| – Intelligence | – Modesty | – Practicality |
| – Intensity | – Motivation | – Pragmatism |
| – Intimacy | – Mysteriousness | – Precision |
| – Intrepidness | – Neatness | – Preparedness |
| – Introversion | – Nerve | – Presence |
| – Intuition | – Obedience | – Privacy |
| – Intuitiveness | – Open-mindedness | – Proactivity |
| – Inventiveness | – Openness | – Professionalism |
| – Investing | – Optimism | – Prosperity |
| – Joy | – Order | – Prudence |
| – Judiciousness | – Organization | – Punctuality |
| – Justice | – Originality | – Purity |
| – Keenness | – Outlandishness | – Realism |
| – Kindness | – Outrageousness | – Reason |
| – Knowledge | – Passion | – Reasonableness |
| – Leadership | – Peace | – Recognition |
| – Learning | – Perceptiveness | – Recreation |
| – Liberation | – Perfection | – Refinement |
| – Liberty | – Perkiness | – Reflection |
| – Liveliness | – Perseverance | – Relaxation |
| – Logic | – Persistence | – Reliability |
| – Longevity | – Persuasiveness | – Religiousness |
| – Love | – Philanthropy | – Resilience |
| – Loyalty | – Piety | – Resolution |
| – Majesty | – Playfulness | – Resolve |
| – Making a difference | – Pleasantness | – Resourcefulness |
| – Mastery | – Pleasure | – Respect |
| – Maturity | – Poise | – Rest |
| – Meekness | – Polish | – Restraint |

(*continued*)

**TABLE 7.2**  Core Values (Continued)

| | | |
|---|---|---|
| – Reverence | – Spirituality | – Unity |
| – Richness | – Spontaneity | – Usefulness |
| – Rigor | – Spunk | – Utility |
| – Sacredness | – Stability | – Valor |
| – Sacrifice | – Stealth | – Variety |
| – Sagacity | – Stillness | – Victory |
| – Saintliness | – Strength | – Vigor |
| – Sanguinity | – Structure | – Virtue |
| – Satisfaction | – Success | – Vision |
| – Security | – Support | – Vitality |
| – Self-control | – Supremacy | – Vivacity |
| – Selflessness | – Surprise | – Warmth |
| – Self-reliance | – Sympathy | – Watchfulness |
| – Sensitivity | – Synergy | – Wealth |
| – Sensuality | – Teamwork | – Willfulness |
| – Serenity | – Temperance | – Willingness |
| – Service | – Thankfulness | – Winning |
| – Sexuality | – Thoroughness | – Wisdom |
| – Sharing | – Thoughtfulness | – Wittiness |
| – Shrewdness | – Thrift | – Wonder |
| – Significance | – Tidiness | – Youthfulness |
| – Silence | – Timeliness | – Zeal |
| – Silliness | – Traditionalism | – _____ |
| – Simplicity | – Tranquility | – _____ |
| – Sincerity | – Transcendence | – _____ |
| – Skillfulness | – Trust | – _____ |
| – Solidarity | – Trustworthiness | – _____ |
| – Solitude | – Truth | – _____ |
| – Soundness | – Understanding | – _____ |
| – Speed | – Unflappability | – |
| – Spirit | – Uniqueness | |

**TABLE 7.3**   Top Seven Values

| Values | Rank |
|--------|------|
|        |      |
|        |      |
|        |      |
|        |      |
|        |      |
|        |      |
|        |      |

choose: these top seven values are those that you remember most often as you go through life. Rank these seven values in order of importance; the most important go first.

Look at your list now. Your top three should be nonnegotiable.

> *Who you are is often defined by the values you will defend.*
> *Our core values are those that we absolutely cannot*
> *negotiate, cannot compromise.*
>
> —The Authors

The intention of this exercise is for you—and you alone—to find out more, better, and entirely who you really are when nobody is looking. Who you are inside, under all the layers of politeness, socialization, training, schooling, education, survival, love, and lacking the one "you" who will always be inside your head, resisting or helping you through your thoughts and actions in life. The one "you" who remembers and feels everything you have ever been through.

Personal values are implicitly related to choice; they guide our decisions by allowing for a comparison between one choice and our associated value with that choice. In essence, our values drive our thinking, feeling, speaking, and behavior.

Some people live strictly according to their values, while others are more lenient. Which type are you?

Maybe this is not something you want to do: determine which values are the ones you would live by. But that's a value, not wanting to adhere to any kind of guideline or rule. Personal values that are developed early in life are resistant to change; they may be derived from particular groups or systems, such as culture, religion, and even political party. But if you ever thought of changing the way you live your life, the place to start is by examining what you would need to value to get what you want. If you are experiencing unease or demotivation in your life or work, it is probably because you are not living according to your values.

Stephen Covey talks about beginning with the end in mind and invites us to consider what it would be like to attend our own funeral and listen to what people would say about us. Chances are that what is said will relate to the values you live your life by. Recently coauthor Andrew was called substantive (real and meaningful) and perspicacious (having insight and understanding things) by two people he respected; he realized that being real and trying to understand things are two values that very much drive his life.

What will people say about you?

## VALUES IN ACTION EQUAL STRENGTHS

Researchers in positive psychology have been looking at how using our values as strengths allows us to be happier and more effective.

Dr. Martin Seligman explains in his book *Authentic Happiness* what is required for genuine happiness to occur:

- **Pleasure.** Positive subjective experience, gratitude, elevation, optimism, faith, and pleasant sensory experiences.

- **Engagement.** Positive experiences of absorption in daily living—at work, in play, and in relationships; using strengths to connect with others.

- **Meaning.** The relationship of oneself to the larger universe; contributing to the common good; living a purposeful life.

If you are not happy, perhaps you can identify what on this list is not happening for you. If you are not living according to your values, you will be unhappy or demotivated. Another reason for being unhappy and ineffective is to not play to your strengths.

Finding values is usually a personal journey, but using your strengths, or encouraging team members to use theirs, makes a tangible difference in the workplace. Management guru Peter Drucker said it this way: "Few managers know their strengths, and yet it is only from our strengths that we make a difference."

## SELF-DISCOVERY EXERCISE

Here is another exercise in self-discovery, from Ryan M. Niemiec, Psy.D., an educator from the VIA Institute on Character. For each of the following questions, check as many answers as you like.

**Wisdom and Knowledge**

Which of these character strengths best describe(s) you?

___ Creativity (originality, thinking of novel ways to do things)

___ Curiosity (interest, openness to experience, novelty-seeking, exploring and discovering)

___ Open-mindedness (critical thinking, judgment, thinking things through)

___ Love of learning (mastering new skills and topics, adding to what you know)

___ Perspective (wisdom, providing counsel to others, taking in the "bigger picture")

**Courage**

Which of these character strengths best describe(s) you?

___ Bravery (valor, not shrinking from difficulties, challenges, or pain)

___ Perseverance (persistence, industry, finishing what you start, going through obstacles)

___ Honesty (integrity, authenticity, taking responsibility for your feelings and actions)

___ Zest (vitality, approaching life with enthusiasm and vigor, feeling "alive")

**Humanity**

Which of these character strengths best describe(s) you?

___ Love (capacity to love, be loved, and be close to others; valuing close relationships)

___ Kindness (generosity, compassion, altruism, being nice, helping/taking care of others)

___ Social intelligence (aware of emotions and motives of others, knowing how to fit in)

**Justice**

Which of these character strengths best describe(s) you?

___ Teamwork (citizenship, loyalty to a group, social justice, working well in a group)

___ Fairness (not letting feelings bias decisions, giving others a fair chance)

___ Leadership (encouraging, organizing, and getting things done in a group)

**Temperance**

Which of these character strengths best describe(s) you?

___ Forgiveness/mercy (accepting shortcomings, giving second chances, nonvengeful)

___ Modesty/humility (not seeing self as more special, letting success speak as is)

___ Prudence (being careful about one's choices, not taking extra risks)

___ Self-regulation (self-control of feelings and actions, disciplined)

**Transcendence**

Which of these character strengths best describe(s) you?

___ Appreciation of beauty and excellence (awe/wonder for art, science, nature, daily life)

___ Gratitude (aware of and thankful for good things that happen, expressing thanks)

___ Hope (optimism, future-minded, expecting and working toward a best possible future)

___ Humor (playfulness, seeing the light side, enjoying laughter, bringing smiles to others)

___ Spirituality/religiousness (faith, purpose, meaning, having beliefs about the universe)

Now from the list above, pick what you believe to be your top five strengths.

1. _____

2. _____

3. _____

4. _____

5. _____

## SIGNATURE STRENGTHS

Are you surprised by the answers in the previous exercise? Or do they confirm what you have always believed?

Are you comfortable expressing these strengths? Does your current occupation allow you to do so?

Coauthor Andrew's top strengths are love of learning, zest, and perspective. So it is little wonder that he enjoys teaching and coaching people. Coauthor Ana's top strengths are bravery, perseverance, and fairness, which equip her to be a strong researcher and advocate for seeking and understanding the truth about people and life.

Living based on your signature strengths is the most powerful way to find happiness and fulfillment!

You may be curious as to why the strengths in the previous exercise were grouped under six categories (wisdom and knowledge, courage, humanity, justice, temperance, and transcendence). This is because Drs. Seligman and Peterson and a team of social scientists engaged in a study of world religions, philosophies, and psychology looking for agreed-upon human virtues. Virtues are core characteristics valued by religious thinkers and moral philosophers. The team discovered that there exist six virtues that transcend geography, time, and culture. The six virtues are wisdom and knowledge, courage, humanity, justice, temperance, and transcendence. These universal virtues are grounded in biology as a means of solving important tasks necessary for the survival of the species. Each one of our human strengths is part of a virtue.

If you want to find out more about strengths and virtues, the authors recommend you visit http://viacharacter.org/.

## WHAT CAN YOU DO?

Now that you know what you value and what your strengths are, you can reflect on how you can apply them. Our skills and talents give us the power to affect the world around us. Sometimes it is worth taking inventory of our skills and talents so that we feel confident and empowered to make a difference. Table 7.4 is by no means an exhaustive list, but it will give you a start on what you can do. Check among all the answers those that apply to you.

With a strong sense of who you are and what you can do, you are then ready to consider who you *want to be.*

## BEST POSSIBLE SELF-LEADERSHIP EXERCISE

A critical self-leadership skill is the ability to motivate yourself to do what is necessary to succeed. To build a strong motivational propulsion system requires tapping into your mind's powerful ability to *visualize.*

Imagine yourself in two to five years from now. Imagine that your hopes and dreams are realized and you have all of the things that are important to you.

Now spend a few minutes describing this life on paper. After free-writing for about 10 minutes, reflect on the values that this visualized life represents. Consider, are you dedicated to becoming this person? Are you willing to do whatever it takes to do so?

## SELF-MOTIVATION

Sports coaches want to motivate their teams, and managers want to motivate their employees, but in reality motivation is an inside job. If you try to motivate others, the effect is not permanent unless those people are inspired to motivate themselves from that point on.

Self-motivation provides the emotional and physical energy for us to take action to achieve our goals and be our best possible self. How we motivate ourselves is linked to our personality and

**TABLE 7.4**   Inventory of Skills and Talents

| | | |
|---|---|---|
| – Administration | – Follow instructions | – Public speaking |
| – Advise people | – Gain confidence | – Raise funds |
| – Analyze situations | – Generate new | – Read |
| – Apply information | business | – Research |
| – Assemble things | – Handle complaints | – See different points |
| – Audit | – Imagine | of view |
| – Bring people | possibilities | – Sell |
| together | – Implement | – Set goals |
| – Budget | procedures | – Sort data |
| – Calculate | – Inspect things | – Summarize |
| – Coach people | – Interpret | information |
| – Communicate | information | – Take action |
| effectively | – Interpret | – Work with your |
| – Comprehend the | languages | hands |
| complex | – Interview people | – Write |
| – Create ideas | – Invent things | – Write reports |
| – Customer service | – Lead people | – Recognize problems |
| – Decision making | – Listen | – Relate to people |
| – Delegate tasks | – Manage finances | – Serve others |
| – Distribute | – Manage systems | – Set standards |
| products | – Meet deadlines | – Troubleshoot |
| – Draw plans and | – Motivate people | – Visualize |
| diagrams | – Negotiate | – Work well in a team |
| – Drive | – Organize | – _____ |
| – Edit | – Perform | – _____ |
| – Enforce rules and | – Persuade | – _____ |
| policy | – Plan meetings/ | |
| – Entertain | events | |
| – Evaluate | – Prioritize tasks | |
| performance | – Problem solving | |
| – Find answers | | |

values. They can be focused primarily on what we want or on what we don't want.

Motivation, self or otherwise, occurs when we have the emotional energy to move away from what we don't want and are strongly drawn to what we do want. If we only want to move away from what we don't want but do not have a clear picture of our destination, we are likely to make bad choices. Also, if we have an idea about what we do want but are still in our comfort zone doing what we are doing, nothing will change.

If you now add intention and meaning to your values, you have a powerful psychological goal-setting mechanism.

## GOAL SETTING

When you have a clearly defined intention, you gain a laserlike focus and begin to take action. Effective execution occurs when intentions are transformed into well-thought-out behaviors. People can often read your intentions, but the world rewards your effective execution. Here are four questions to ask yourself:

- "What is it I want to do?"

- "What actions do I need to take?"

- "What will the effect of those actions be?"

- "Will these effects be in line with my intention?"

Self-leaders set goals for themselves; through self-observation and self-feedback they regularly achieve them. Because self-leaders know what their values are, their goals will be intentional.

What goals are you working on at the moment? Are they specific and measurable? The process shown in Table 7.5 will make this goal a part of your "self" so that you will work on it unconsciously.

**TABLE 7.5** Goal-Setting Process

| | |
|---|---|
| 1. State the outcome in positive terms. | What do you want to move away from? What do you want to positively and intentionally achieve or experience? (Desired state) Where are you now? (Present state) |
| 2. Visualize your goal. | What will you see, hear, and feel when you have achieved your goal? Can you taste it? |
| 3. Be specific. | When will you achieve this goal? Where will you be? Who will be there? |
| 4. Break it down into actions. | What are the steps or stages involved in reaching this goal? Have you broken each step down to a specific action or set of actions that are within your control? What are these actions? If there are actions required that are outside of your control, can you influence people to get them done? |
| 5. Identify roadblocks. | Does anything prevent you from achieving this goal? Is this a reality or just your belief? Has anyone else achieved this goal? What did he or she do? What do you need to believe to achieve this goal? |
| 6. Create an end point. | How will you know that the goal has been achieved? When will you feel satisfied? How will you celebrate or reward yourself for achieving this goal? |
| 7. Get motivated. | How bad do you want it? Can you feel this goal pulling on you? Have you told other people you have committed to achieving the goal? Reward yourself for hitting milestones toward the goal. |

**TABLE 7.6**  My Goals

| | |
|---|---|
| 1 | |
| 2 | |
| 3 | |
| 4 | |
| 5 | |
| 6 | |
| 7 | |

Now write out your own goals (see Table 7.6).

So, now you know who you are, what you can do, and where you are going. Other parts of this book cover influencing your communication and behavior on the way to getting there.

## Summary of the Chapter

Many of us live a great part of our lives—some our *entire* lives—believing that we don't fit or that we are not good enough because we are judged by traits and qualities that are not natural to us. In this chapter you are encouraged to find out all you can about your personality and how you function best. For all of us, knowing our strengths and what we value gives us more confidence and clarifies our contribution to our own lives and to the lives of those around us.

When we act according to our values, we act strongly and inspire others to do the same. The tools in this chapter are essential for you to start defining what your goals in life are and building your flexibility and self-motivation to pursue them.

# Self-Leadership
# Strategies Defined

*The first and best victory is to conquer self.*
—PLATO

A mong the main factors that prompted the authors to write this book, two were probably the most important: (1) our belief that self-leadership can be learned, and (2) our enthusiasm and responsibility toward spreading the word—and the advantages—of self-leadership to as many people as possible.

Both of us were in perfect agreement to the point that we didn't want to create another prescriptive leadership recipe that says, "Leaders must do *X*, *Y*, and *Z*." We share the understanding that there isn't only one way of being a self-leader or leader; so we didn't want to write a book that would say things such as, "Self-leaders always know what to do," "Self-leaders are always confident and have high self-esteem," or, "Self-leaders always know how to guide others to become self-leaders as well." Both of us have struggled to find and live with self-leadership, and we empathize with you if sometimes you struggle with your emotions, lack confidence, or reach a point in your life where you are confused about what direction to take. These things are normal and human and don't prevent you from developing your self-leadership.

Becoming a self-leader is a daily decision that a person makes; there's always the possibility of choosing not to exercise responsibility. Do we recommend you do that? Not at all, mainly because we like what practicing self-leadership did for us, for our lives, and for those around us. But we both know that it can be hard sometimes, challenging, and a lot of work when, at times, all people would like to do is to rest their souls, or let their "inner child" search for somebody to parent them and tell them that everything is going to be okay and that they don't need to do anything.

Self-leaders are not perfect; they are authentic. They are not confident or happy all the time, but they own their emotions, good or bad, and take feedback and make adjustments. Regular practice moves self-leaders toward greater self-awareness, for being at peace with themselves and for being capable of thinking clearly and making sound personal decisions no matter what is going on inside or outside of them.

This chapter explores strategies: the thoughts, behaviors, steps, and actions each of us can take to become a practicing self-leader. The term "practicing self-leader," which has been used in past chapters, reminds us that self-leadership is indeed a daily practice, one in which no one can become very proficient. Nevertheless, it's a practice, a continuous never-ending process. Its specific steps are not always easy to do, but they are possible and attainable.

As the great strategist Sun Tzu said some 2,500 years ago: "The good commander seeks virtues and goes about disciplining himself according to the laws so as to affect control over his own success."

## STRATEGIES

We all have the power to choose our own thoughts and feelings and not be a slave to them. From owning and choosing our thoughts and feelings, we become purposeful with our speech and actions. As we receive feedback on our speech and actions we can check these against our intentions and goals and make adjustments if required.

Of course, this is sometimes easier said than done. If, for example, you did not have an upbringing that encouraged self-leadership, or if you are experiencing stress at work, with finances, or in a relationship, then you will need some strategies to gain and maintain control.

Finding the right strategy or combination of strategies that works for you may take some trial and error. If you are reading this book on the suggestion of your coach, counselor, or mentor, then you might get some perspective from them on what to use. The authors highly recommend that you get a dedicated journal to capture your thoughts, beliefs, triggers, and results as you start your journey toward self-leadership mastery.

You might be pleasantly surprised that you are already practicing some of the strategies, and this ought to encourage you to continue to fine-tune them and perhaps add to your repertoire.

There are three main sets of self-leadership strategies: constructive thought strategies, behavior-focused strategies, and natural rewards strategies (Manz and Neck 2004; Neck and Houghton 2006; Prussia et al. 1998). Each one has a sequence of behaviors and actions. Each one is explained in the paragraphs that follow.

## CONSTRUCTIVE THOUGHTS, OR MENTAL STRATEGIES

> *Whatever you do, or dream you can, begin it. Boldness has genius and power and magic in it.*
> —JOHANN WOLFGANG VON GOETHE

Constructive thought strategies deal with changing patterns of thinking, which creates more positive ones. Through mental strategies, negative thought is replaced with optimistic self-talk. There are four mental strategies, or steps, to attain a status of constructive thoughts:

1. Improving our own belief system

2. Using our imagination to facilitate desirable performance

3. Using self-talk to our advantage

4. Learning and using new and improved scripts

Each one of these steps will be explained, and examples will be given, in the paragraphs that follow.

## IMPROVING OUR OWN BELIEF SYSTEM

A belief is an assumed truth that can come from our own experiences or from our blind acceptance of what people tell us (Rokeach 1960). There are several theories about how beliefs are formed inside our minds, but simply put, a belief is an idea or concept that, at some point in our life, we have said yes to or that was confirmed for us during our early imprinting by our parents or caregivers. Our values, beliefs, and identity are created and function as a mental map (see Chapter 4).

We are more than our beliefs, and yet our beliefs can drive our thinking and behaviors without us even noticing.

Richard Bandler (1985), cofounder of Neuro-Linguistic Programming (NLP), puts it this way:

> Behaviors are organized around some very durable things called beliefs. A belief tends to be much more universal and categorical than an understanding. Existing beliefs can even prevent a person from considering new evidence or a new belief.

Because our beliefs can be empowering or disempowering it is an essential first step that we step back and examine our beliefs and even our beliefs about our beliefs and assess how they are impacting our life. This activity can be done alone or with a coach or trusted friend.

Here is a quick place to start: circle the letter of the beliefs that you hold.

a. I'm too old to change.

b. It's better to keep quiet than to be thought a fool.

c. There's no failure, only feedback for improvement.

d. If someone is nice to me, it means they want something.

e. I have to know the right people to get ahead in life.

f. The world is abundant; there is plenty for everybody.

g. I am more than my behaviors.

h. My culture defines who I am.

i. I can't lose weight.

j. If I get serious, I get stupid.

If you circled (a), you hold a belief that change is over for you, and that will create a self-fulfilling prophecy. This belief may originate in the fact that as we get older we have more time to reinforce existing behavior patterns. Nevertheless, there are people who have changed their minds and their behaviors well into their eighties, and so this is not a fact but a belief. It will only create a fact if we believe it.

If you circled (b), your belief has probably been programmed by your culture/parents or you have had a painful experience of speaking up and being ridiculed. Of course, modesty and humility are great qualities, but what if you have something important to say? Will this belief prevent you from having a voice? Have you kept quiet at a cost to yourself and your authenticity?

If you circled (c), then you hold a belief that will allow you to learn and grow. This belief helps you not to think you are a failure when things go wrong; instead, it propels you to adjust your behavior and persist.

If you circled (d), then you may believe yourself unworthy of receiving appreciation or love from others. Yes, it is true that some people will be nice to you in order to win favor or influence you, but others see the value in who you are and are willing to express it. In addition, if you hold onto this belief it may prevent you being nice to others in return.

If you circled (e), then your belief probably has been formed by observation of how the world works or from advice from a significant influencer, such as an early boss. What we need to be aware of here is the belief behind the belief, which could be self-limiting. If you believe you don't have the right connections and cannot make them, then you could erroneously conclude that you can't get on in life.

If you circled (f), you are opening yourself to opportunities and are unlikely to experience jealousy or a scarcity mentality. Of course, this belief may leave you vulnerable if you are working in a context with greedy and unscrupulous people, but as a self-leader you would probably extricate yourself from such a situation.

If you circled (g), then you believe in your ability to change. Many people believe that we are defined by what we do or what we have done, but, if you look around, there are plenty of examples of people who have realized that the past does not equal the future and have made a significant life change.

If you chose (h), that is understandable (see Chapter 9 for a discussion of cultural influences); however, if you feel out of alignment with the culture into which you were born or in which you work, you can choose to change yourself or the culture.

If you chose (i), you have fully ascribed to a self-limiting belief that could include "I can't stop smoking" (or drinking, swearing, procrastinating) and a host of other excuses.

> *If you want to, you will find a way; if you don't want to,*
> *you will find an excuse.*
>
> —JIM ROHN

If you chose (j), then you have realized that a sense of lightness or humor will allow you some flexibility to see things with a different perspective. Because self-leadership is an ongoing process, we must be kind to ourselves and not get too serious, as this will cause stress and limit our options.

Having done this exercise, you will start to be aware of the beliefs that are driving your actions. And if you are not getting the results you want, you can now step back and ask yourself the question, "What belief is driving this?"

Look out for patterns of behaviors or repetitive thoughts. These are clear indicators that there is a belief in play, a belief about ourselves, about other people, and about life itself. Prepare to be courageous and brave, to face ugly truths such as uninvited beliefs that you are not good enough. In the authors' experience, this is actually the most prevalent hidden belief the most people have, deep within: that we are not good enough. This belief can manifest itself in several ways, but they all mean the same thing. For instance, if we consistently deflect relationships from our lives because people occur to us as wanting to take advantage of us, we could be hiding a belief that we are not good enough. How? At a glance, it could seem that we are being careful and responsible. In fact, however, we are actually being fearful of being fooled by those who we believe are smarter than us, because we think that we are not good enough to stand up for ourselves.

As you examine your beliefs, bravely and courageously, think about what their impact is on your life, in your reactions, and in your behaviors. Know that these beliefs are not real; they are not you. If they are really toxic, you might want to explore them with a professional who specializes in this area. Whatever your beliefs are, if they are useful, they can be reinforced; if they do not serve you, they can be challenged and changed.

As discussed, a belief is a frame that governs your experience of the world and your interaction with it. When we say no to a disempowering belief and adopt a new belief we create a "reframe." We create a new script for ourselves (another self-leadership strategy).

The formula for a reframe can be simply: it's not $X$, it's $Y$. Examples include:

It's not a failure, it's a learning experience.

It's not that change is tough; it's that we've changed in the wrong direction.

I'm not worthless; I've just been doing a great job at hiding my value up until now.

The strategy for updating your belief systems is therefore as follows:

1. Identify a belief or beliefs that prevent you from being or doing what you want.

2. Step back from these beliefs and realize that they are not real but have been adopted during your early years or constructed from past experience.

3. Choose to reframe the belief: it's not this, it's that.

4. Say a strong yes to the new belief and begin to take action from this frame of mind.

5. Check for feedback that this new belief is moving you toward your goal.

When identifying a limiting belief, be aware that you could be three or four beliefs (sometimes more) back from your original thought about an experience. The object of the exercise is to find the core belief that is driving your behavior.

When you find the core belief, you can then ask yourself the question, "Is believing this serving me?" If the answer is no, then you can consider, "What would I need to believe to get the results I want?" Another question could be, "What else could be possible for me to believe about this?" If this new belief is safe for you and for those around you, then you can start to say yes to this belief. Try it on. You can always come back for another analysis. Once you have identified a new and resourceful belief, you can turn it into a motto or a mantra so that it becomes part of you and you will start getting results from the actions that emerge from this belief.

## USING IMAGINATION TO FACILITATE DESIRABLE PERFORMANCE

In Chapter 7 you were encouraged to imagine your "best possible self"; this is an example of using your imagination to facilitate desirable performance. Elite athletes use positive visualization to achieve their goal, and you can too.

This technique works because your physiology responds to what you are imagining or remembering as if it is happening right now. And if your physiology has rehearsed a performance, it will perform close to prediction at the required time.

To be a self-leader it is essential to gain control of your imagination, because whether you are imagining good things or bad, you are setting up a self-fulfilling prophecy.

Here's how to do it:

1. Imagine the scene where you desire to perform well: your office, your boss's office, your home, and so on.

2. Add as much detail as you can remember or imagine about this scene: key objects, colors, sounds, textures, and smells.

3. See yourself in the scene as if you are watching yourself in a movie. See yourself as the person for whom this task is "no problem": confident, composed, and prepared.

4. Add any other people who will be present. Imagine them as friendly and open to your ideas or actions.

5. Play the scene in your mind as if you were watching a movie that has you as the lead character. Direct the movie and adjust the dialogue so that it plays the way you want it to go.

6. When you are happy, then you have the movie just right. Step into the movie so that you are experiencing it as if it were happening right now. Be aware of how it feels to perform the way you desire; notice your breathing, your posture, and what it is like to see through the eyes of a performer.

7. Repeat this visualization regularly until you are ready to perform.

Try this example now. Imagine you want to ask for support or even a raise from your boss. Play the scene in your mind. Vividly imagine the dialogues you will go through, always putting a winning twist on them to your advantage. Even if you imagine that your boss's first reaction may not be a positive one, picture how you will handle his or her negativity. Envision different outcomes of this conversation, and prepare yourself mentally to handle whatever comes out of the conversation. What this exercise will do for you is get you prepared and knowledgeable, mentally in control of whatever happens in this conversation. Nothing will catch you off guard. You own your reactions the minute you start visualizing them in advance.

As mentioned, social learning theory teaches us that we learn through imitation of others. We can therefore model the performance of others and add their behaviors to our visualization. Early in his career as a conference speaker, coauthor Andrew would watch great speakers and observe how they moved on stage and handled the audience. He would then visualize and rehearse using the same techniques with an imaginary audience of his own. When it came time to perform, he was able to move on stage and connect effortlessly. What is it that you need to perform? Take a moment to visualize your best possible performance.

## USING SELF-TALK TO ADVANTAGE

Do you have a coach, mentor, or wise friend? Do you feel good when that person speaks to you in a tone that encourages you? Of course you do. What about a critic, a person who constantly judges you and points out your faults and tears you down? We certainly hope you'll answer "no" to this choice when the time comes for you to seek advice, friendship, or encouragement. And yet many people we know actually do like to have others criticize them.

Coach and critic can be people in our lives, but it could also be that we have them installed in the "software" of our mind. They communicate to us through our self-talk, so talking to yourself, either silently or aloud, is not odd behavior but rather a perfectly natural and powerful strategy for self-leadership. It is interesting that we can be a wise and strong advocate for the right actions and behaviors in others but completely forget to direct this powerful energy and strategic component to ourselves. Self-leaders can choose to self-talk and self-coach themselves to winning attitudes.

There is a strong effect upon our minds that comes from listening to our own voice saying confident, encouraging words to ourselves. When we dare to say out loud the coaching we need to hear and have always wanted to hear but no one has ever given us, we are doing something that in psychology is called "positive self-parenting."

Self-parenting is those inner conversations and internal dialogues we all carry on continuously. Our mind is continuously processing thoughts and feelings in what could seem like an internal dialogue of sorts. This dialogue is actually conducted between our inner child and our inner parent—and for the great majority of us it goes unidentified through life. Pollard (1992) explained that our inner parent is the internal voice that expresses the programming we received from our parents until we reached the age of seven. It's the voice we use for rational thinking and decision making. Our inner child is the voice that expresses enthusiasm, needs, and desires; it's the voice with which we experience pleasures and joys. We reproduce internally, unknowingly, the pattern of relationship we had with our parents. If this pattern was a positive one, our internal conversations between inner child and inner parent will be positive. If that relationship was a negative one, we will have negative inner dialogues. Pollard (1992) defended practicing and developing positive patterns of self-parenting, one that actually will help us build self-esteem, foster our self-motivation to pursue our goals, and achieve the life we want.

The mental strategy of using self-talk to our own advantage builds on positive self-parenting. It encourages us to be as positive with ourselves—encouraging, supporting, and remaining loyal—as we are outwardly to our friends and others when we are comforting and encouraging them (i.e., being the best friends—and parents—ever). This self-leadership strategy tells us to be good to ourselves first. (Remember the airplane rule: put the mask in yourself first, and then—only then—help someone else.)

Coauthor Andrew has experienced setbacks in his life where he needed to take control of his self-talk, as he relates:

> In 2001 due to circumstance beyond my control, and some bad decisions by me in response to these, I lost my business, my money, money properties, and my cars. I was in debt with no assets and no job or business. If you have experienced this, you know that your "inner critic" can run wild, but after a couple of weeks of feeling sad for myself, I started to coach myself back. I told myself I had skills and knowledge and experience and that there would be people who needed these and would pay for them. I started calling organization after organization and offering my services. Initially I met with lots of rejection, but I kept coaching myself through self-talk that I would find an opportunity and, sure enough, I did. I found one company that was prepared to pay me for some consulting, and then another, and leveraging the testimonials for these I began to build a business which today lets me speak and coach around the world.
>
> More recently I faced a new challenge, because life's like that; the woman I love decided that there were some things about me that she didn't like, and she questioned whether we should stay in the relationship. This took me completely

by surprise (we often miss what is under our noses), and I responded in shock and then with anger. The voice of my "inner child" screamed at how this was unfair and how it was not getting its needs met. I was out of control and in pain, and, although I understood what was going on, I could not stop the negative critic and the tendency to blame. My self-awareness let me know that this was one of those occasions where I needed some professional help, and after a couple of sessions my "adult" inner voice began to take control. I was able to still the child and begin the work required to rebuild the most important relationship in my life.

One thing that this recent experience has taught me is that our friends and colleagues may offer advice in difficult situations, but we are the only ones who can help ourselves to be and to do what we need to be and to do.

The authors recommend that you start to notice your inner dialogue. Ask yourself the question, "What do I need to say to myself to get the results I want?" Then start saying those things to yourself in a tone that puts you in the frame of mind to take action.

If you notice that certain things trigger you, then you can prepare a phrase to say to yourself. For example, when a colleague is rude or criticizes your work, you can say to yourself, "Interesting feedback; what can I learn from this?" This approach allows us to get feedback for our blind spots and not react emotionally to perceived criticism.

Nike, the sports shoe people, coined a fantastic self-talk phrase: "Just do it." There are many phrases that you can choose to say to yourself, such as:

- "I can learn this; I am learning this."

- "I can focus; I am focused."

- "I can make the time; I am making the time."

- "I can learn from this; I am using this feedback."

- "I am valuable."

- "I am growing in confidence."

- "Each action brings me closer to my goal."

Now come up with a few of your own.

## LEARNING AND USING NEW AND IMPROVED SCRIPTS

Once you are aware of your self-talk, it is relatively easy to spot your own faulty thoughts or outlook, but there is an unconscious process that is much harder to get a handle on because it feels like reality.

If your life were a play or a movie, what kind would it be? Action, drama, romantic, tragedy, adventure?

Our lives, like a play or a movie, have a script (or, for that matter, a book: we are sure you have heard somebody say, "I am starting a new chapter of my life"). And this is an important realization: we are not just actors on the stage of our life (as Shakespeare would have us believe); we are also the author and director of our life. Motivational speaker Anthony Robbins is fond of saying, "The past does not equal the future"; this strategy is the key to writing the future you want.

As mentioned, for most people scripts are an automatic sequence of behaviors that they practice unconsciously, or out of awareness, over and over again. We can become locked into our stories; they become us, and they define us . . . and become self-fulfilling prophecies unless we wake up and make a choice.

We create successful scripts and unsuccessful scripts. (Some scripts that worked in the past may not work for us anymore.) If we are living on automatic mode, just repeating things without even thinking because that's what we know how to do, this repetition will go unnoticed.

For example, someone has been betrayed more than once in sentimental relationships. At each betrayal, the chances that the experience will repeat itself become higher, as that person enters relationships with that fear in mind. The fear triggers certain behaviors in both participants of the relationship that could contribute to take it to a path of betrayal or something similar. We continually run scripts from the past in our mind—after all, that's how we learn about life, right? We observe what has happened in similar situations in the past, and we try to predict the outcomes—avoiding, if possible, the bad outcomes and fostering the good ones.

If we have had bad experiences in the past, those events can become scripts that we follow unconsciously, driving us to the same outcomes we experienced before. Two or more people can be running scripts that interact, creating a "toxic dance" or "powerful synergy." When we step back from our own lives, we can begin to observe the games we have been playing that are driven by these scripts.

> *The definition of insanity is doing the same thing over and over and over and expecting different results.*
> —BENJAMIN FRANKLIN
> (OFTEN MISATTRIBUTED TO ALBERT EINSTEIN)

Catching the scripts that have been running our lives takes a self-observation (a behavioral strategy) or feedback from a coach, but once you catch or recognize the script and the game it is creating, you can choose to modify your script and therefore your behavior and your results. The mistake most people make is to assign blame or to try and change others. Having a choice, a saying on how your life will go from now on, is a very powerful and enticing thing!

The authors invite you, now, to examine your life, your difficult moments, looking for things that happen often and situations that repeat. Where you find these, you will find a script right there, running your life. Scripts can also be in unsuspected places, such as in your beliefs about yourself. For instance, many of us feel insecure when interviewing for jobs. There's a script right there that we may not be looking *good enough* for the position or that we may not be able to perform the work.

When you observe a pattern, and identify the script you can ask yourself the following questions:

- "What is the script I am playing?"

- "Is this script empowering or serving me?"

- "Where did it come from?"

- "Does it have any value now?"

- "What script would empower me?"

- "Will I choose to apply the new script?"

It takes practice to make a new script, so you will need to cue yourself a few times until it becomes your natural way of being.

An interesting study at Ohio State University in 2009 found that people who were told to sit up straight were more likely to believe their own thoughts than those who slouch in the chair (Briñol, Petty, and Wagner 2009). The authors believe that this illustrates the role of physiology in performance, as described in Chapter 6 in the exercise "Accessing and Amplifying Confidence."

*Whatever you conceive and believe, you can achieve.*
—NAPOLEAN HILL, *THINK AND GROW RICH*

Whatever you tell yourself, do it with an attitude of belief. Pretend you are facing a difficult or challenging situation, if you need to, before you actually do. Encourage yourself aloud as you prepare.

## BEHAVIORAL STRATEGIES

> *Not being able to govern events, I govern myself.*
> —MICHEL DE MONTAIGNE
> (FRENCH WRITER, 1533–1592)

Behavior-focused strategies focus not only on behaviors but also on self-awareness. As you started your self-leadership journey through exploring who you are, you probably started noticing your most typical behaviors. Some of them might have guaranteed you some personal success so far, while others should definitely be changed. There are five behavioral strategies that can help us control our actions (Neck and Houghton 2006):

1. Self-observation

2. Self-goal setting

3. Self-reward

4. Self-correction

5. Cues management

## SELF-OBSERVATION

> *Why should we not calmly and patiently review our own thoughts, and thoroughly examine and see what these appearances in us really are?*
> —PLATO

Self-leadership begins with self-observation, which means noticing our thoughts, feelings, and behaviors. With self-observation we shift our focus from everyone else's actions and pay attention to what we ourselves do, how we react to people and to things and events.

The process of self-observation is like the checking of the instruments of an airplane to ensure it is flying level and on course. By checking in on ourselves we can notice what triggers reactions from ourselves and to other people. That will allow us to make adjustments that allow us to be more purposeful and effective.

As described earlier in the chapter, it is through self-observation that we are able to catch our beliefs, understand what we have been saying (self-talking) to ourselves, and identify the scripts that are running our lives.

Self-observation, also known as introspection, contemplation, or self-reflection, is simple but not always easy. When we observe, we find it difficult not to judge, and self-judgment can be painful. That's because so many of us have been taught or conditioned in childhood that we are not good, that we are lacking so many traits, and/or that we are not good enough. And that makes us very reluctant to look at ourselves.

Self-observation should not be confused with our superego, the judging or controlling part of our mind, which may have been programmed by authority figures or religion to shame us and cause us to feel guilty when we have certain thoughts. Many religions have a very limited application of self-observation; because they "know" what's right and wrong, they have a list of sinful thoughts, feelings, and behaviors to look out for (see Chapter 10). This is not the same type of self-observation being discussed here. The authors are proposing a *guilt-free* self-observation.

In a self-leadership context, self-observation is about making a commitment to learn the truth about ourselves and our world, no matter what it is. This requires comparing, but not judging, our thoughts, feelings, and behaviors with feedback we get from the world around us. That way, we don't get caught up in our own fantasies and biases.

Self-observation is about when, why, and under what condition we exhibit certain behaviors. Here are questions to ask yourself:

- "What do I think, feel about this?"

- "How is my body responding [to stress, relaxation, pleasure, and so on]?"

- "What am I paying attention to?"

- "What am I paying undue attention to?"

- "What are my distractions?"

- "What are my biases?"

- "What am I unaware of?"

- "Am I focused on problems or opportunities?"

This strategy is about how we run our psychological machinery. We must inquire: "What's going on?" "What's behind that?" "What else can I learn about this?" This inquiry must be undertaken with the commitment to accept whatever we learn about ourselves. To quote a maxim: the truth will set you free.

For example, recently coauthor Andrew was in a meeting with a potential client for his consulting services. The client had kept him waiting, shown him into an interview room, and then said, "Tell me about yourself." Andrew asked if he or anyone in the company had heard of his work or read the biographical data that had been sent to them. He responded with, "No, we are just looking for some vendors." At this point Andrew felt himself becoming angry and indignant, and he noticed the muscles of his jaw tensing and his mouth becoming dry. Through self-observation he noted that his ego had been threatened and that he had been labeled a "vendor" when he preferred to work as a partner in creating solutions. Self-observation allowed him to notice all of this before engaging in a behavior that would have guaranteed him not to get the contract. He was first able to run a script to shift his thinking and feeling to a calmer place and build rapport, resulting in his getting the piece of business.

So, how do you become good at self-observation? Isn't it likely to lead to being self-obsessed? To become good at self-observation requires practice—the practice to check in nonjudgmentally.

Try this exercise: look at your watch for five minutes without distraction. You will probably find doing so quite challenging because you experience all sorts of distractions and make judgments such as "This is taking a long time," "Has my watched stopped?," "This is a waste of time," and so on.

Now spend five minutes just sitting and observing the world around you, and accept every little thing that comes along without judgment. You might hear the ticking of a clock or the hum of an air conditioner or feel how the chair is supporting you and whether you are moving to get comfortable. As you notice all the sensory data that comes your way, just accept it as information without judgment.

Practice this regularly, especially when you notice you are feeling stressed. Start with observing: What am I thinking about this? What am I feeling about this? What are my behavioral choices about this?

Some people find it useful to keep a journal about the frequency, duration, and triggers of undesirable behaviors. Through self-observation you may find yourself making some changes to your actions and reactions or you will be ready to apply other self-leadership strategies.

As you start practicing self-observation, you will start noticing one of the miracles of self-leadership: you won't be as obsessed about how others should change to meet your needs because you are focused on yourself, on how you can live better with what you have and what you are.

Remember:

*An unexamined life is not worth living.*

—SOCRATES

## SELF–GOAL SETTING

A core element of self-leadership is that we know where we are going; self–goal setting is the strategy for directionalizing, motivating, and keeping ourselves accountable (i.e., keeping our commitments).

Ways to apply this strategy are discussed in Chapter 7; however, as this is such an important activity, the authors would like to add the following.

Self–goal setting doesn't need to be about a huge, once-in-a-lifetime goal; you can set a series of small goals or medium-size ones or intermediate ones—whatever it is you need to attain temporarily or forever. If you do have a "big, hairy, audacious goal" that inspires you, then you can divide it into steps and make each step a goal in itself. It is important that you obtain early successes so that you build up your self-confidence.

Goals need to be attainable. And what is not attainable for self-leaders? Almost nothing, as people can reach almost whatever they put themselves to reach. For instance, if coauthor Ana made a goal to be an astronaut, she would have to be ready to study physics and engineering, to train and exercise for the exhaustive physical exertion that such a mission involves, to start contacts with space agencies around the world that could accept her in their program, and be ready to spend some serious money to begin with. One thing that could impede her from reaching such a goal would be her age: Is there an age limit for those untrained to become an astronaut? If there is one, this would be an unattainable goal, unworthy to spend time and energy pursuing. Thankfully, Ana's goals are more Earth-bound.

But what about you? Have you thought already of something you would like to reach? To have more personal control of your own temper? To stop drinking? To learn another language?

Setting a goal doesn't mean that you have to accomplish it alone. You can surround yourself with experts, coaches, teachers, trainers, or whomever you need to accomplish it. Self-leadership is having the initiative to pursue whatever you need to do in life, from the goals that you set for yourself to business goals your company sets up for you. Goals have to be personal for you. The authors encourage you to try on small goals first, so that you can build successes to fuel you up to more challenging and difficult goals.

> *Whatever you can dream, begin to do it. Boldness has power and magic in it.*
>
> —GOETHE

Tell people whom you trust about your goals; start doing something, even small little steps. Bring to fruition, somehow, something, so that your goal starts moving closer to you.

One of Theodore Roosevelt's most famous quotes was, "Do what you can, with what you have, where you are." Bring into the physical realm your thoughts, your dreams, and your goals, and see how they transform the world around you.

## Self-Reward and Self-Correction

The third and fourth behavioral strategies—self-reward and self-correction—are essential to the practice of self-leadership. They help the self-leadership practitioner to disengage from the need for recognition coming from others and start acting as her or his own personal motivator. For these two behavioral strategies to work well for you, you will need to identify your most motivating objects, thoughts, and images and your most rewarding behaviors and attitudes.

That's what you will use to praise yourself when you finally accomplish each one of your goals. Specifically for the fourth behavioral strategy, self-correction, you should remove or withhold those same rewards, or even establish a purpose of working harder, if a previously set plan of action for your goal has not been fulfilled.

An example of self-reward could be treating yourself to a movie, a good healthy meal, an affordable shopping spree, or even a day to rest. Examples of self-correction could be working a few hours longer if you got distracted along the way to completing a task, postponing partying or relaxation until tasks get finished, or going an extra mile to make something important work.

Self-correction means doing what we say we will do, and being someone whom others can count on. This means sticking to our commitment and responsibility, no matter the cost of it.

As an example, coauthor Ana, during the course of her graduate studies, had many opportunities to practice self-reward and self-correction. If she failed in getting one of her research phases done, she would stay longer at the graduate office, spending the weekend doing the extra work needed. As she finished chapters of her master's thesis or doctoral dissertation, she would treat herself to an ice-cream cone or a movie, the only things that a not-wealthy graduate student could afford. The success of this effort could be measured both by her obtaining her degrees and by some extra pounds that she gained during her graduate years. Since then, she avoids suggesting the ice-cream reward . . . but strongly emphasizes the success rate of the strategy!

What goal are you working on at the moment? How will you reward yourself as you hit milestones toward this goal? How will you correct yourself if you do not do what you say you will?

## CUES MANAGEMENT

Cues management deals with using reminders and attention focusers to help identify important moments, benchmarks, in tasks. Self-leadership researchers recommend that you write down and post lists of priorities to organize your daily activities and then set cues such as signs in the working area, bracelets, rings, or any objects that can help you focus on these tasks.

Cues can be about behaviors or attitudes. The Lance Armstrong Foundation sells bracelets with the slogan "Live Strong" to remind cancer sufferers to maintain a positive attitude.

As well as identifying positive cues, you can eliminate negative cues in your working area, such as sources of noise and distraction, and disengage from those people who disrupt your productivity.

Coauthor Ana once advised a student who constantly failed in meeting deadlines, was always late for appointments, and couldn't get tasks fully completed as agreed. This student, let's call him "Mike," had a small but mighty group of friends with whom he would meet in sports bars. As good as these friends may have looked to Mike, they were actually derailing him from the pursuit of an important goal in his own life: obtaining his master's degree. Through several conversations, Mike became aware that if he wanted to get this one academic goal completed, he would have to deemphasize, even if for only a few months, the friendship with this group. Doing this was very difficult for him, as he learned to rely on these friends as a substitute for his family, living far away. Interestingly, Mike was very bright and could have conducted his graduate course seamlessly. His difficulties were coming from his personal life, not from his intellectual or academic life. Eventually he was able to disengage from the group and successfully completed his master's. But we all knew it was a painful—although necessary—step in reaching his goal.

As you start working on self-observation and develop good insights about how you function, reflect on what hinders you and what your strengths are; you can build your tasks using this knowledge to maximize your power to accomplish your goals. For instance, the more you know yourself, the more you will know what stops you, what distracts you from your tasks, and the more you can prepare yourself accordingly for when those distracters happen. In fact, self-knowledge is one of the most important bases for both self-leadership and leadership (see Chapter 7). With self-knowledge, you can identify your most common pitfalls and be prepared for them and address them so that they won't harm your accomplishments.

## COGNITIVE OR NATURAL REWARDS STRATEGY

Natural reward strategies are enjoyable features that we can build into our regular or challenging activities, as a way to make the tasks look naturally rewarding (Manz and Neck 2004). By identifying and enhancing natural reward on tasks, not only do we make them more pleasant to be accomplished but we will also experience an increase in intrinsic motivation, self-determination, and feelings of competence (Deci and Ryan 1985; Neck and Houghton 2006).

Here are a few ways by which we can increase tasks' natural rewards:

1. Determine places where the task can be performed in a more pleasant way.

2. Identify activities that can be built into the tasks that could make work naturally rewarding.

3. Redesign tasks to incorporate places (contexts) and activities that make them more pleasant to be accomplished.

4. Identify the task's pleasant aspects, and focus your thoughts on those aspects rather than on the unpleasant ones.

5. Distinguish and focus on rewards that are actually part of the tasks, separating them from those you built in. Celebrate both!

6. Develop the habit of focusing on the pleasant aspects.

To use a personal example, as coauthor Andrew was approaching the deadline for this book he was able to schedule some mornings writing at poolside in a green and leafy environment. He would invigorate himself with a swim, write or edit a section of the manuscript, and then reward himself with another dip in the pool, a coffee, or, as a special treat, a fresh croissant.

During the same period, coauthor Ana resorted to her favorite self-reward: watching movies. She would check movie schedules and plan a session *only if* she finished her self-given assignment.

It's not about avoiding or ignoring the difficult and distasteful aspects of the tasks; rather, it's about dealing with them constructively (Manz 1990a). For instance, working on a detailed business report can be, for many people, a boring and tiring thing to do.

Personally, some people may like the description part of the report, and others prefer to work with the numbers. When applying the natural rewards strategy, each one of these types of people could emphasize the part that they like to do more, celebrating and enhancing that part. They could also use that particular piece of work as a reward for having to deal with the less personally pleasant part. They could also include celebrations for finishing the difficult parts or, midway through them, give themselves small rewards for completing it within the allotted time frame or, better yet, for finishing it earlier.

We all have things in life that we don't like to do, and yet we have to deal with them. Learning how to use the natural rewards strategy helps us beyond working hours, and well into our personal lives, when many times we have to deal with hard moments, difficult situations, and tough things to do. With the natural rewards strategy we learn to focus on the positive aspects of everything—there always are some positive ones as well as negative ones.

## NONPRESCRIPTION

As emphasized in the beginning of this chapter, the authors do not intend to have this book be rigidly prescriptive. Rather, we wanted to share a method through which everyone can live a more fulfilling, conscious, and accomplished life.

Table 8.1 summarizes the strategies discussed in this chapter. These can be used alone or in combination with one another—one at a time, all at once, whatever way they fit better in your life and help you get a good grasp at your inner life. That is, after all, all we really have and can count on. Keep in mind: people who act irresponsibly or disconnectedly can end up losing the support of even their most beloved ones. Self-leadership—and self-leadership strategies—help all of us get our act together, live connectedly,

**TABLE 8.1**  Summary of Strategies

| 1. Mental Strategies | |
|---|---|
| Improving belief system | ■ Identify a belief or beliefs that prevent you from being or doing what you want. |
| | ■ Step back from these beliefs and realize that they are not real. Say no to the old belief. |
| | ■ Choose to reframe the belief: it's not this, it's that. |
| | ■ Say a strong yes to the new belief and begin to take action from this frame of mind. |
| | ■ Check for feedback that this new belief is moving you toward your goal. |
| Using imagination | ■ Imagine the scene where you desire to perform well. |
| | ■ Add as much detail as you can remember or imagine about this scene. |
| | ■ See yourself in the scene as if you were watching yourself in a movie. Be the person for whom this task is "no problem." |
| | ■ Add any other people who will be present. Imagine them as friendly and open to your ideas or actions. |
| | ■ Play the scene in your mind as if you were watching a movie with yourself as the lead character. Direct the movie, and adjust the dialogue. |
| | ■ When you are happy that you have the movie just right, step into the movie so that you are experiencing as if it were happening right now. |
| | ■ Repeat this visualization regularly until you need to perform. |

(continued)

**TABLE 8.1**   Summary of Strategies (Continued)

| 1. Mental Strategies | |
| --- | --- |
| Using self-talk | <ul><li>Identify what you are currently saying to yourself.</li><li>Ask, "What do I need to say to myself to get the results I want?"</li><li>Say it to yourself in an encouraging tone.</li></ul> |
| Living with improved scripts | <ul><li>Use self-observation or a coach to catch the scripts that are running your life.</li><li>When you observe a pattern, and identify the script, you can ask yourself the following questions:<br>– "What is the script I am playing?"<br>– "Is this script empowering or serving me?"<br>– "Where did it come from?"<br>– "Does it have any value now?"<br>– "What script would empower me?"<br>– "Will I choose to apply the new script?"</li><li>Get the new script into your physiology (see Chapter 6).</li></ul> |
| **2. Behavioral Strategies** | |
| Self-observation | Regularly ask yourself the following questions:<ul><li>"What do I think [or feel] about this?"</li><li>"How is my body responding [stress, relaxation, pleasure, etc.]?"</li><li>"What am I paying attention to?"</li><li>"What am I paying undue attention to?"</li><li>"What are my distractions?"</li></ul> |

**TABLE 8.1**   Summary of Strategies (Continued)

| 2. Behavioral Strategies | |
| --- | --- |
| | ■ "What are my biases?" |
| | ■ "What am I unaware of?" |
| | ■ "Am I focused on problems or opportunities?" |
| Self–goal setting (see Chapter 6) | ■ State the outcome in positive terms. |
| | ■ Visualize your goal. |
| | ■ Be specific. |
| | ■ Break it down into actions. |
| | ■ Identify roadblocks. |
| | ■ Create an end point. |
| | ■ Get motivated. |
| Self-reward | ■ Identify thoughts, speech, and behaviors, such as milestones toward your goal, that need reinforcing. |
| | ■ Give yourself permission to do something pleasurable when you achieve any of the above. |
| Self-correction | ■ When you do not behave as you have committed to, withhold rewards and redouble your effort to achieve your commitments. |
| Cues management | ■ Use reminders to focus on important behaviors and tasks. |
| | ■ Remove distractions. |

| 3. Natural Rewards Strategy | |
| --- | --- |
| | ■ Find places to perform the task in a more pleasant way. |
| | ■ Identify activities that can be built into the tasks that could make work naturally rewarding. |

*(continued)*

**TABLE 8.1**   Summary of Strategies (Continued)

| 3. Natural Rewards Strategy |
| --- |
| ▪ Redesign tasks to incorporate places (contexts) and activities that make them more pleasant to be accomplished.<br>▪ Identify the task's pleasant aspects, and focus your thoughts on those aspects rather than on the unpleasant ones.<br>▪ Distinguish and focus on rewards that are actually part of the tasks, separating them from those you built in. Celebrate both!<br>▪ Develop the habit of focusing on the pleasant aspects. |

live a life of purpose, carry our own weight, and hopefully inspire others to do just the same.

The practice of self-leadership allows us to maximize our power of choice over events. As Viktor Frankl said in his book *Man's Search for Meaning* (1963), we have the ultimate call of choice and power in our lives: to decide how we will react to events. That's what self-leadership strategies give to us: tools to live our life in personal freedom, responsibility, and self-determination.

## CHAPTER 9

# Organizational Self-Leadership

> *When the leader's job is finished, the people say,*
> *"We did it ourselves."*
>
> —LAO TZU

An organization with a culture of self-leadership will have a competitive advantage in terms of creativity, innovation, and customer experience.

The authors understand that this is a bold claim, but we have witnessed these results when an organization takes the challenge to embrace self-leadership. In this chapter we share our experiences with companies that have pioneered self-leadership and show you how you can adopt this approach in your own organization.

Unfortunately, many organizational cultures, while espousing the benefits of empowerment and self-direction, inadvertently discourage many self-leadership behaviors. This is because most businesses today are driven primarily to achieve short-term financial goals, which tends to create an environment where people are afraid to fail. In this fear-based environment, managers default to a command-and-control leadership style, telling employees what to think and do.

In a self-leadership culture, the reverse is true. In fact, the language of self-leadership is, "Ask, don't tell." This approach is possible when the organization's leadership accepts that they do not have to have all the answers and recognizes that there is a pool of untapped intelligence and innovation within the workforce. When people are invited to contribute and to solve their own issues as well as the organization's challenges, they experience an increase in self-awareness, self-responsibility, and self-motivation. For an organization to "walk the talk" of self-leadership, the senior leaders must consistently take the "ask, don't tell" approach. There is an interesting paradox here, because you cannot tell leaders, "Ask, don't tell." Rather, you have to invite them to discover the power of this approach. (For more on coaching and leading with self-leadership, see Chapter 11.)

The authors have witnessed many self-leadership interventions struggle to take root in terms of instilling long-term behavioral change. This is primarily because the managers who have been exposed to self-leadership practices have returned to the workplace with little or no support for their new behaviors. There is a difference between learning something on a program and applying these new behaviors in real time and within the confines of a stressful business environment. People will naturally default to their old ways if there is insufficient support and validation of the new behaviors and continued reward for short-term results.

The command-and-control style does have its place. Imagine traveling on an airplane and the oxygen masks drop from the ceiling and you experience a sudden loss of altitude. What if then the captain comes out of the cockpit and says, "Okay, ladies and gentlemen, obviously we have a bit of a problem, and I would like to get your input and ideas about the best way to handle this"? To illustrate with a personal example, coauthor Andrew worked with officers of Singapore's Airport Emergency Service, an organization with a very strong command-and-control operating style, for this very reason. It struggled with the idea of self-leadership, but eventually it came to appreciate the benefit of developing self-leaders during training and drills so that they could improve reaction times and decision making under pressure. When a plane was in trouble, the command-and-control reflexes kicked in, and lives were saved.

A self-leadership culture has empowering leaders and employees who exercise their autonomy in line with the organization's mission, vision, values, and strategy (see Chapter 11). Figure 9.1 shows the results of different levels of empowerment and employee autonomy.

People who work under a leader who is very direct or who live or work in a country or company with an authoritarian culture will have difficulty expressing autonomy in terms of speaking up, making decisions, and being creative and innovative. They may just accept this command-and-control style. Or perhaps, if they desire to exercise a higher level of autonomy and are not given the space to

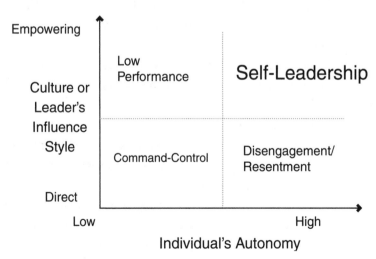

**FIGURE 9.1** Self-leadership Culture Model.

explore that, they will become disengaged at work or resentful of their leader or culture.

Much human resources research has shown that disengaged employees are less productive whereas engaged employees generate more profit, are more customer focused, work more safely, and are more likely to stay with the organization (Wollard 2011). Co-author Ana has conducted extensive research with employee engagement in a medical center. She found that when employees can be part of the decision making, contributing to the ideas that will be put to practice, they own the place, they own their actions, and they personally embrace customer satisfaction as their own personal goal. The best-performing companies know that improving employee engagement and linking it with the achievement of the company's overall goals will help them win in the marketplace.

On the other hand, if a leader or culture is empowering but individuals have low autonomy or refuse to exercise autonomy, the likely result will be low performance as the employees wait for instructions or complain about a lack of direction. The authors have witnessed this when Western managers take over a team of Asian employees who have been conditioned to not make their own decisions. The Western manager will often become frustrated with the low performance from his or her employees and then switch to a command-and-control style rather than coaching for increased self-leadership.

Self-leadership flourishes when there is an open culture or empowering leadership style and individuals can and want to exercise autonomy. Along with this come the associated benefits of increased creativity, innovation, and productivity.

Teams function more effectively when individuals exercise self-leadership, taking responsibility *for* their own thoughts and feelings and being responsible *to* the group's shared goals and objectives (see Chapter 11).

The authors propose that self-leadership should be the foundation of any organizational development program. To skip the self-leadership piece is to leave out a significant part of developing a learning organization, as you can see from Figure 9.2.

Self-leadership and personal leadership are synonymous, and the authors' research and practice have shown that organizations that encourage and facilitate the behaviors described in this book have more effective leaders. Those people have the ability to spot and respond to opportunities, and they possess the resilience to cope with change. In the modern turbulent business environment, the ability to lead change is a strategic imperative. To lead change, business leaders must be able to see opportunities and manage resources while planning for multiple eventualities.

Self-leaders are more empathetic and understanding of what drives others, and therefore they can be more inspirational leaders. Because they encourage others to access their own self-leadership, the operation will be more effective overall, even through periods of change.

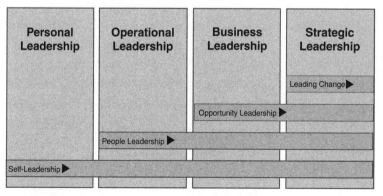

**FIGURE 9.2** Self-Leadership as a Foundation for Leadership Development.

Coauthor Andrew has worked with the managing director for Merck Ltd. in India, Dr. Marek Dziki. Dr. Dziki is committed to creating results for his organization while simultaneously developing his people. He is passionate about creating strong bench strength at multiple levels of his management team. Starting with Dr. Dziki's direct reports, we began the process of creating a self-leadership culture by conducting a number of sessions to facilitate the application of self-leadership to oneself and to leading people.

With the help of human resources, Dr. Dziki picked a group of senior managers subordinate to his management team who were dubbed "GenNext leaders." The GenNext leaders attended quarterly off-site trainings covering self-leadership, people leadership, opportunity leadership, and leading change. Each GenNext manager was trained to coach self-leadership in his own teams.

By committing to this process, Merck India had the talent to cope with and prosper through the aftermath of the recent financial crisis. It also could adapt to a changing business environment and have leaders ready to step into more challenging roles during a reorganization as well as a merger and acquisition.

The process of working with the lead and cascading the process down has proved to be the most successful model and has been applied with the Rogers Group, a Mauritius-based multinational organization. Rogers has many divisions that include logistics, hotels, property, travel, and aviation. Working with the CEO and the human resources director Manish Bundhun, the team from Self Leadership International (Andrew's consulting company) created a self-leadership culture with the executive team and then ran sessions with each division. It was extremely gratifying to watch members of the executive team attend these sessions and begin to coach their people on how to apply the principles. Manish also set about exposing the entire organization to self-leadership principles through one-on-ones and leadership forums. The economic climate has not been kind to Mauritius, and yet Rogers is investing in people to remain competitive.

To prevent leaders from returning to command-and-control behaviors it is important that they be coached or supported when they return to the workplace from a training session or off-site.

Coauthor Andrew has been introducing self-leadership concepts as part of a Management Excellence program at Microsoft Asia Pacific. To ensure that people felt supported and were able to open up, Self Leadership International introduced and facilitated cross-functional action learning teams. Action learning is a process developed by Reg Revans (1980, 1982, 1998) in which leaders can share with peers from other functions and be coached without fear of being judged. There is a strong link between self-leadership and empowerment.

Pat Sheehan, a human resources consultant who specializes in empowerment and works with us at Self Leadership International, shares the following:

> Active employee involvement is essential to the continued success of the modern organisation. When we intend to implement anything new that involves or impacts the employees, there is a simple rule to ensure the success of the implementation: *tell them what is going to happen, invite their participation, encourage their critique—positive and negative— implement with their involvement, and after the implementation ask them how we did.*

Is there a magic formula for creating a self-leadership culture and therefore a high-performance workplace? The authors' experience is that you must take a holistic or systems approach. Figure 9.3 identifies parts of the system that can be leveraged to create lasting change.

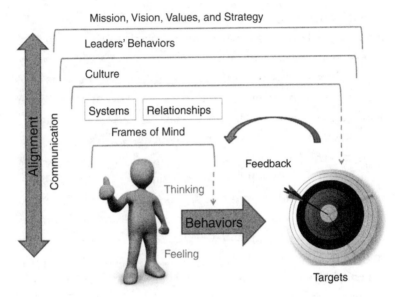

**FIGURE 9.3** Systems Approach to Self-Leadership to Create an Environment of Lasting Change.

The following explains each of these components, in turn:

1. **Mission, vision, values, and strategy.** Ideally, all change should cascade from this element. When an organization has done the work to identify and communicate these four elements, everybody knows why the organizational system exists, where it is going, what is important (how to behave on the way), and how to get there (with a "road map").

2. **Leaders' behaviors.** The leaders of the organization must "walk the talk" of the mission, vision, values, and strategy. They must communicate through word and deed so that there is alignment.

3. **Culture.** The collective beliefs and values of the people within the organization are its culture. The culture can

be tangible or intangible, and it informs people what is the "right way" to speak and act within the organization. *Culture* can be synonymous with *environment* in an organizational context and can be identified by asking such questions as, "Is this a good place to work?," "Am I respected here?," and "Does my effort make a difference?"

4. **Systems.** The various processes, rules, and regulations that enable or disenable work within the organization are its systems. How people are remunerated, rewarded, and validated plays a very important role in how they perform. A major demotivator will be if people do not understand the reason for the systems or consider them to be unfair.

5. **Relationships** include boss, peer-to-peer, internal and external clients, and subordinates. Relationships are influenced by culture and are evident by the quality of communication, collaboration, and teamwork within the organization.

6. The **frame of mind** of the people within the organization consists of their values, beliefs, intention, and identity. In a high-performance work culture, people's values are aligned with those of the organization. Behaviors in terms of what people say and do and how they say and do them are driven by what they think and feel, which result from their frames of mind. Disengaged people often behave in a way that is not in alignment with the company's values because they themselves are consciously or unconsciously not in alignment with them.

7. **Targets** and goals must be clearly set and communicated so that people within the organization know what is expected of them and how they will be measured. In a

self-leadership culture, people know why they are doing what they are doing, because self-leaders operate intentionally.

8. **Feedback** is essential across the system. Self-leaders will seek feedback on how they are doing relative to their intentions, values, and beliefs. They, in turn, will be able to give feedback to others on how those people are aligned with the team or organization's mission, vision, values, and strategy.

As Figure 9.3 illustrates, the higher frames of mission, vision, and values should cascade down through leadership behaviors to create an environment for self-leadership to flourish; therefore, to create change in an organization with low self-leadership it is advisable to start from the top down, although doing so is not always possible.

Choosing what interventions to apply to improve self-leadership may be decided by observing symptoms, such as people lacking motivation, initiative, or the will to speak up; and/or you can conduct a cultural survey. At Self Leadership International we have developed a tool to assess which leadership and self-leadership behaviors are absent or present in an organization's culture; using this tool allows us to identify which elements of the system need the most attention.

If you are in a leadership position within your organization, then the information and models described here will be useful; however, you may be working as an individual contributor or only have a small team reporting to you. If you are an individual contributor, then applying the strategies described in Chapter 8 will enable you to influence yourself and be a role model to others; if you lead a small team, then you can do the same thing and begin coaching your people to apply self-leadership (see Chapter 11). Whatever you choose to do, do not underestimate the influence power of self-leadership.

Coauthor Andrew, who has experienced more than one-on-one self-leadership coaching sessions, cautions that those sessions not become therapy sessions; there is always the risk of that happening. The fine line is the action. Each one of us has to pursue his or her psychological well-being with the help of an appropriate professional. Self-leadership coaches will help you to get the steps and the actions accomplished.

## THE LARGER CULTURAL FRAME

The system shown in Figure 9.3 is missing some frames. These include the country and dominant ethnicity where the organization was founded. These external cultural factors will influence the organization's mission and vision and ways in which they will be executed.

The authors have witnessed and researched the effect of culture on the expression of self-leadership. Before sharing our observations we must concede that by definition they are generalizations; organizations, groups, and individuals may differ.

Self-leadership is a Western term (Adler 1997), yet the concepts of self-awareness and self-development are firmly rooted in Eastern culture. Alves and others (2006) affirmed that the understanding of self-leadership is universal but that its intrinsic building concepts of self-efficacy and intrinsic motivation depend on levels of autonomy and leadership styles, all of which in turn depend on cultural dimensions.

It has been said that Western society strives to find and prove "the truth" and is more action and results oriented, whereas Eastern society is more interested in finding balance. In effect, you might say, this is the difference between human *being* and human *doing*.

> *The superior man understands what is right; the inferior man understands what will sell.*
>
> —Confucius

Eastern cultures are generally much more collective and collaborative whereas Western cultures are typically more individualistic. Chapter 3 discussed the need for people to balance their focus between "self" and "other." Just as individuals need to differentiate between the self and other and find a balance, so do organizations. Genuine self-leadership organizations need to find a balance between collective (Eastern) culture and individualistic (Western) culture. Unfortunately, when it comes to entrepreneurship, change, and innovation, the two styles do not blend so easily, as the Eastern view is on stability whereas the Western one focuses on rapid change.

Self-leadership researchers around the world, including the authors, are dedicated to exploring how the concept of self-leadership applies to and is understood in different cultures. A useful model for understanding the effect of culture on organizational and individual behavior is Hofstede's culture dimensions (see Figure 9.4). The following paragraphs explain each of the components of the model.

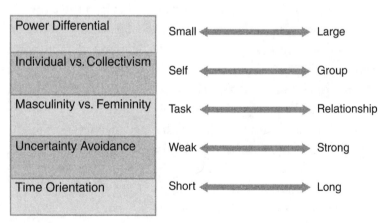

**FIGURE 9.4** Hofstede's Culture Dimensions.

People are much more likely to demonstrate self-leadership behavior overtly when the *power* difference between them and their boss or bosses is low. High-power differential cultures almost always involve the command-and-control style already described.

In cultures that are focused on *individualism* it is easy to observe the self-leadership—or the lack of it! In more collective cultures, on the other hand, self-leadership is demonstrated in a group setting, which leads to team potency (see Chapter 11).

Large Western organizations have been historically "*masculine*" in style, focusing on the task and getting the job done at the expense of the more "feminine" values of relationship and intuition. With more women leaders taking senior roles and a recognition of the benefits of a "balanced" approach, the authors hope that a shift will occur. In fact, coauthor Ana has defended that the new management style is neither masculine nor feminine, but it's an androgynous style, that is, a style that combines the best traits of each gender and goes beyond the limitations of genderized discussions to dedicate instead at improving everybody, regardless of gender and sexual orientation (Kazan et al., 1998).

Organizations with rigid standard operating procedures and an inability to change are demonstrating strong *uncertainty avoidance*. Companies that are nimble and rapidly adapt to changing circumstances have weak uncertainty avoidance; this flexibility can be exciting to some, but it can also be quite disturbing for individuals whose personality is more procedural (see Chapter 7).

Some companies in the East, particularly in Japan, used to have 50-year strategic plans; nowadays, in the West the focus is often reduced to the next quarter's financial results. It used to be that strategic plans were made for 5 or 10 years. This is no longer true, particularly after the worldwide economic and financial crisis of 2008. In the new norm it has become difficult to have long-term focus. The authors hope that, for the sake of our children and the planet, this situation can change.

As an exercise, place an alphabetical letter *a* or *b* on each of Hofstede's continuums in Figure 9.4, indicating whether it applies to (a) your country or to (b) your organization.

In another perspective on culture, Ho and Nesbitt (2008) noted that in Chinese culture the self-leadership practice of self-observation is not directly linked to the task but to relationships during the execution of tasks. This means that generally for Chinese cultures, relationships and collaboration are at the heart of tasks rather than separate from them. Coauthor Andrew has noted this when conducting interviews and performance reviews in Asia. When a candidate or employee is asked to describe what he or she has *personally* done, that person answers with, "We did . . ." So it becomes very difficult to determine that individual's contribution to any given outcome or specific result.

An interesting study by Curral and Marques-Quinteiro (2009) conducted in Portugal found that self-leadership, self-efficacy, and intrinsic motivations are dependent on autonomy levels and leadership style, which is exactly what we have shown in Figure 9.1. This study did not set out to analyze cultural differences, but it has shown that autonomy and leadership are strong culturally related concepts that must be taken into account.

We often hear that "self-leadership won't work in this culture." Nevertheless, Chaijukul (2010) examined self-leadership in the context of Thai private organizations in Bangkok (577 employees of private companies in Thailand) and found that self-leadership strategies had the same effect in the group studied in terms of motivating work performance, enhancing self-efficacy, improving self-motivation, and giving job satisfaction as had been asserted in other studies in the United States. Typically, Thais are known to be non-confrontational and reluctant to say no or to speak up, but this study shows that self-leadership does work in Asia.

More research is being conducted to understand how self-leadership works in different parts of the world. For example, coauthor Ana is investigating self-leadership in Brazil. Researchers, professors, and respected self-leadership authors Jeffrey Houghton, from West Virginia University, and Christopher Neck, from Arizona State University, have opened a research site to study self-leadership worldwide; anyone can participate. Their web address is http://be.wvu.edu/information_technology/survey/surveyHome.htm. The authors of this book encourage you to access the research site and complete the self-leadership questionnaire posted there. Not only will you be contributing to the international understanding of self-leadership but you will also receive your own self-leadership report, with possible areas for improvement to reach optimum personal and professional self-efficacy.

## Summary of the Chapter

To change means to be challenged, whether at the individual or the organizational level. When people are invited to contribute and to solve their own issues as well as the organization's challenges, they experience an increase in self-awareness, self-responsibility, and self-motivation. In organizations, this practice needs to have the support of all leadership levels. That commitment guarantees that people who have been exposed to self-leadership practices don't naturally default to their old ways. (They might do so if they feel that there is insufficient support and validation of the new behaviors and if rewards are continued for short-term results.)

Organizations that encourage and facilitate the behaviors described in this book have more effective people leaders than those that don't. These people have the ability to spot and respond to opportunities, and they possess the resilience to cope with change. In the modern turbulent business environment, the ability to lead change is a strategic imperative.

Just as it happens individually, organizations are influenced by their country's culture and/or dominant ethnicity. That in turn will influence how self-leadership is understood and practiced and how self-leaders will translate and execute the organization's mission and vision. Many researchers around the world investigate culture's impact on self-leadership, and they affirm that its concepts and positive applications are universal.

## CHAPTER 10

# Transcending with Self-Leadership

> *The dogmas of the quiet past are*
> *inadequate to the stormy present....*
> *As our case is new, so we must*
> *think anew, act anew.*
>
> —ABRAHAM LINCOLN

It has been said that we are living in a new normal; after the 2008 worldwide economic and financial crisis we are all navigating through unchartered waters. The recent past has not prepared us to live what we are living now, and this is true whether we are in Brazil, Singapore, the United States, Australia, Europe, or wherever.

> *Owners of capital will stimulate the working class to buy more*
> *and more expensive goods, houses and technology, pushing*
> *them to take more and more expensive credit, until their debt*
> *becomes unbearable. The unpaid debt will lead to bankruptcy*
> *of banks, which will have to be nationalized, and the State*
> *will have to take the road which will eventually lead to*
> *communism.*
>
> —KARL MARX, *Das Kapital* (1867)

Despite the predictions of Karl Marx and other futurists, the vast majority of us were lulled into a false sense of security. We never imagined the challenges we are now facing with jobs, currencies, healthcare, security, and conflict. How do we now plan for our future when we have no idea what it will be? And to make things even more challenging, because of the incredible advances in communication technology, nowadays we immediately experience every crisis wherever it happens in the world, live, in full color, and with tangible despair. In such times, how are we to be fulfilled rather than just survive? The answer is to transcend, to rise above the negativity by living with mindfulness and purpose.

Philosopher Peter Singer (1995) suggested that the only thing that is strong enough to maintain our will to live fully through these changing times is the pursuit of personal ethics. Defining ethics is a task for several books, but what is meant here is the study of moral codes, of what is good and right to do, how to behave correctly, and how to face the world and the people around us. Personal ethics specifically is living by values (see Chapter 7) that encompass not only our own personal interests but also the interests of other living creatures and the environment around us. Stated another way, it's about being unselfish, being aware that we share our existence and the means for it with everybody and everything else around us; our own personal interests are important but not above the interests of everyone else.

The authors agree with Singer and believe the strength and conviction required to pursue personal ethics can be fostered from within through the practice of self-leadership. We believe that in self-leadership lies the possibility of finding new answers and new ways of dealing with life's challenges. These answers are not yet known for problems no one has seen before; they need to be discovered. This is a fluid new normal, where each person needs to count at least on him- or herself to face the myriad of situations, problems, and circumstances for which he or she has not been prepared.

On a deep, personal level, only you can know what you are thinking and feeling and how you want to react to what is happening around you. By embracing the self-leadership paradigm, which says that our thoughts can be controlled, each of us is able to filter through a torrent of undesirable and self-defeating thoughts, selecting those that she or he wants to follow and the beliefs to adopt. With self-leadership we all become psychologically adults; thus, we no longer have to operate blindly from the fears of an inner child or programs instilled by parents, teachers, or early authority figures. We choose to stay in control by using our self-leadership strategies.

At work, in business, and in our families all of us can choose to just survive or we can opt to transcend the challenges and live and work with meaning and purpose.

## SELF-LEADERSHIP AND SPIRITUALITY

It is now a common practice for people to refer to themselves as "spiritual but not religious." Often, this identification doesn't mean necessarily a rejection of organized religions, but it's recognition that they are seeking a higher truth, self-improvement, even enlightenment. After all, spirituality is an anthropological phenomenon by which people try to understand their connection to and place within the universe, a way for many people to find meaning and purpose in life (Smyth, 2010).

Being "spiritual" is being in a search for the peace and serenity that ultimately come from within. People who claim to be "spiritual" very often embrace continuous improvement and lifelong learning and seek inner peace through self-attention and discipline. The process is the same for self-leadership.

Both spirituality and self-leadership foster the ability to see the "big picture" when the difficulties of daily living obfuscate one's discernment. Spirituality and self-leadership help people understand their connectedness with each other, while at the same time acknowledging their own responsibility in improving themselves to contribute to the overall good.

If self-leadership is the science of thought and behavior control, aimed at fulfilling one's purpose in life, spirituality is—for those who feel the need to embrace it—an effective complementary tool that can help further enhance the new resilience gained through self-leadership. Spirituality is thus complementary, not opposite, to self-leadership.

## TRANSCENDING WITH SELF-LEADERSHIP IN THE WORKPLACE

For managers and workplace leaders, self-leadership points to empowering relationships, fostering people's development, and enhancing their abilities. Author Joan Marques interviewed over 100 leaders in for-profit and nonprofit settings, looking for ideas on the requirements to be a successful twenty-first-century leader. She came up with these characteristics of what she called the "awakened leader":

- Adaptable to different circumstances

- Driven

- Passionate and committed to achieving his or her goals

- Resilient

- Capable of using failures as lessons for growth

- Having a clear vision of the bigger picture and the future

- Clear when formulating his or her own values

Marques says that awakened leaders, through learning with their flaws, develop their emotional intelligence, which enables them to relate—with compassion—to even the most oppressed among their followers. Awakened leaders share qualities such as courage, inspiration, and the ability to instigate positive change.

The authors cannot help but see similarities with self-leadership, as Marques (2010) further describes each of the awakened qualities. For instance, achieving awakening requires people to realize that they can change only their own lives; that is, they can adapt to different circumstances but not force others to do the same. Self-leadership is the science—and the art—of knowing the steps to promote necessary changes in ourselves to achieve the goals we need to achieve. In self-leadership there are clearly established steps that will help take us to the new levels and paths where we need to be (see Chapter 8).

Self-leadership's strategies include self-knowledge, self-reflection, and self-observation to help us shape our behavior in necessary ways to achieve what we perceive as necessary and unavoidable. Marques says that "wakefulness is acquired through thinking, feeling, observing, experiencing, learning and unlearning, in other words, by living" (2010, p. 8). Specifically, behavioral self-leadership strategies emphasize self-observation, discipline, self-reward, and self-correction when appropriate (see Chapter 8).

Wakefulness requires the ability of letting go—that is, unlearning and releasing things and thoughts that misguide us. Let's compare this goal with self-leadership's mental strategies. Mental strategies aim at helping all of us promote changes we need in ourselves, through examination of our own thoughts and beliefs, looking for the effect on us of these beliefs, and replacing them with new and more effective ones.

Wakefulness requires releasing; that in turn requires courage, for it means that we may have to turn away from certain objects, habits, people, and places. Self-leadership cognitive strategies teach us to surround ourselves with the environment, objects, cues, and people that help us pursue our goals. These strategies teach us how to use what we already know about ourselves to recognize and eventually avoid points that trigger unwanted behaviors.

Are self-leaders the same as *awakened* leaders? Are they our best bet to face the future in front of us? Let us consider this summary definition of all the definitions of leadership: "a relationship between leaders and followers . . . the influence process by which they achieve common goals" (Drath 2008, p. 20). Leadership as influence is much too narrow a definition for the times we are living in now. Drath (2008) said about leadership influence that we all constantly influence each other, and in some instances the strongest influence is even hard to detect. He said that "People are working in contexts in which that asymmetrical influence relationship is absent." (Drath 2008, p. 20).

Examples of teams and places where the relationship between leaders and led are more symmetrical can be found in self-managed teams of professionals, in families with aging parents, where grown-up children are now making the decisions, and/or cross functional task forces where several leaders share leadership, among many other examples.

The kind of leadership we are looking at today, argues Drath, has to look beyond leaders and followers. It has more to do with the ability to produce agreement on the *direction* where we are going, with having a framework for *alignment,* and with developing a sense of *commitment* to the collective work. When there is no leader, how do people get to accomplish what they need to? How is this agreement created? (For more information, see Chapter 9.)

This agreement is created through talking and sharing, through the cycles of suggestion, disagreement, and compromise. The authors believe that through self-leadership a mutual influence can be achieved, helping us all to transcend momentary needs and become self-generators of influence, participation, proactiveness, and efficiency. Self-leaders are self-directed, self-propelled, and adaptable because they seek full collaboration wherever and with whomever they choose. Self-leaders don't need to be convinced, checked upon, and stimulated into action. Wherever they choose to be, they align themselves there, looking for their best tools and skills to do the best work they can do. They choose to participate by themselves and apply what is necessary to accomplish what is needed. They are committed to finding meaning and purpose and therefore to excel in whatever they do.

## WITH SELF-LEADERSHIP, FROM HERE TO BEYOND

The authors passionately believe that self-leadership is an intrinsic part of the new normal all of us are living now. When our past beliefs no longer provide a safe path to guide us through the decisions we have to make, we can only count on solid personal values, on our own, independent ability to reflect, to make things happen, and to make our life move on. If anything can remain solid through the world changes, it is our character manifested through our self-leadership. That will not only guide us through whatever we will undergo but may also inspire others to transcend.

In organizational behavior, an area where self-leadership can have a particularly positive impact, governance is often dependent on human interdependence and trust (Poppo, Zheng, and Sungmin 2007). Self-leadership acts upon both trust and interdependence as it allows people to exercise their true self with peace and dignity, consistently and responsibly.

Self-leadership contributes to the positive organizational scholarship (POS) approach to organizational behavior. One of the premises of POS is the belief that enabling human excellence in organizations fosters the development of people's latent talents; at the same time it reveals hidden possibilities among people and systems, which benefits both humans and organizations (Dutton, Glynn, and Spreitzer 2006).

POS looks at generative dynamics in organizations that contribute to the enhancement of strengths and virtues, resilience and healing, vitality and thriving, and the cultivation of extraordinary states in individuals, groups, and organizations. Self-leadership is a sure, step-by-step, guilt-free, explanatory, and motivating way toward human excellence. Through self-leadership practice and choices, people discover their own latent talents and work on developing them; at the same time, their challenges are managed through thought and behavior control. Self-leadership helps people to define their goals in life; explore their personal virtues, vitality, resilience, and strengths; overcome their difficulties; and become individuals with knowledge-based self-confidence, able to contribute to the creation of dynamic and excellent organizations.

However far we look into the future, it seems certain that all of us will need to be self-reliant, to have the ability to make—individually and collectively—responsible and conscious decisions and follow through with sensible actions. Self-leadership takes us from the very initial steps of self-understanding, from not knowing, through the degrees of understanding, self-control, and consciousness. Self-leadership theory and practice accept that many of us don't know yet what we need to know and what we ought to become, to face what's coming. What it does do, however, is give us, at whichever state of development we are, strategies to grow, develop, and contribute to ourselves and to the world—to transcend.

## Summary of the Chapter

In this chapter we have explored the philosophical questions of "How do we overcome challenges?" and "How do we perform at a higher level?"

We see a common theme in religion and spiritual practices that self-responsibility is a requirement and that "help" will come only when we first take action and correct our failings. The differences seem to lie in whether we adopt a prescribed set of meanings and actions or whether we choose to find our own purpose and ethics.

Coauthor Ana's doctoral research on self-leadership showed that people with better-developed spirituality were also better self-leaders (Kazan, 1999). What we tried to demonstrate here is that self-leadership works hand-in-hand with our most precious beliefs, and in no way or manner contradicts a religious way of life.

## CHAPTER 11

# Leading and Coaching with Self-Leadership

> *Coaching is unlocking a person's potential to maximize their own performance. It is helping them to learn rather than teaching them.*
>
> —TIMOTHY GALLWEY

The focus in this book thus far has been about accessing your own self-leadership, because you have the power to change yourself. But in addition to changing yourself the intent of self-leadership is to positively influence *others around you.*

You can influence people in a number of ways. First, you can be a role model, by walking your talk and demonstrating that it is possible to manage your emotions, communication, and behaviors on the way to achieving your goals. Second, you can coach people to access their own self-leadership; by doing so, you become an empowering leader.

Chapter 9 discussed asking and not telling; this is the principal skill of coaching—asking questions. Coaching is listening, asking questions, and listening to the responses; eventually the coachees hear themselves and reach a point where they can choose how they think, feel, speak, and act. Coaching leads to self-leadership because it assumes these things:

1. People have all the resources to solve their own problems.

2. People are much more likely to follow through on a course of action if they come up with the answer themselves.

Whenever we forget these principles, we can rob people of their chance to exercise self-leadership. When a subordinate comes to us and asks us how to solve a problem and we give them the answer, we set up dependency that hinders them from developing their own problem-solving skills. When we set a goal for someone without first asking that person what he or she would like to stretch for, we take away motivation and commitment.

> *People who are coaches will be the norm. Other people won't get promoted.*
> —JACK WELCH, FORMER CEO, GENERAL ELECTRIC

Earlier chapters discussed the difference between being responsible *for* and being responsible *to*; coaching self-leadership is about facilitating others to take responsibility *for* themselves and their choices, to be clear about the goals and agreements that they are responsible *to*.

Mike Davis, an emotional success coach in the United States, uses the responsibility *for/to* concept when he coaches his clients to use their emotions as their ally rather than their enemy. He relates the following story:

> One couple who asked me to work with them—let's call them George and Mary—came for help because George, the husband, would at times get very angry, yell expletives at his wife, and call her names we won't repeat here! This was dis-

tressing for them as they were a devoutly Christian couple and held positions of leadership in their church.

Because George was the one yelling and cursing at his wife, I decided to work with him first, apart from her.

I first wanted to know what it was that triggered the anger in George. We established that George was triggered by being called "stupid" or "dumb" by his wife when she was upset with him. George reacted with such anger because this is what his alcoholic father called George as a young child. As a young, helpless child, George could do nothing but take the verbal abuse from his father. When his wife called him dumb or stupid, he felt like that little helpless child again being berated and verbally abused by his father, so he lashed out at his wife.

George hated this behavior, as it contradicted his values as a devout Christian and it made him feel like a hypocrite. So he was ready and motivated to change. We first did some work around forgiving his father, and then I coached George and walked him through the Me/Not Me pattern [see Chapter 6]. I had him imagine his wife outside the boundary lines he established and calling him "dumb" and "stupid." As he imagined this, I said to George, "Now this is your space—you can allow her words in or choose not to allow them in; this is your space, and you decide what comes in and what does not." We found it helped George if he gestured his hands forward as if he were pushing out the words and keeping them out of his personal space.

After rehearsing this several times George told me he felt much more in control and realized that his wife's words were *her* words and that he did not have to take them in and make them a part of *his* world. I encouraged George to practice this at least twice a day until our next coaching session in two weeks when I would meet again with him and his wife.

At our next meeting I asked George and his wife how they were doing. George excitedly told me that he had been prac- ticing the Me/Not Me pattern and had not lost his temper, cursed at his wife, or called her names since our last session. I turned to Mary and asked her, "So what has it been like?" Mary told me, "It's true; he's been different. I got mad at him a few times, and he didn't get angry or call me names when I called him dumb."

Mary then said, "The only thing that bothered me is that I noticed that instead of getting angry with me he now gestures with his hands like he's pushing me away or telling me to go away!" George and I both laughed, and I explained to his wife what George was doing. (George had not told her.) She also laughed . . . and then we worked together on her *not* calling George dumb or stupid!

George and Mary are still married at the time of this writ- ing (six years later). George is still maintaining responsibility for his own actions and responses . . . and Mary is no longer calling him dumb!

I am sure you know someone who is making things personal, so how do you get that person to take responsibility—other than giving him or her a copy of this book?

The secret is to ask questions empathetically and without judging. Your line of questioning might go something like, "I no- tice you get angry about $X$. I'm curious that you should choose to be angry about that. Does $X$ have control over you?"

Such a question paces the observable behavior and invites the listener to consider the dynamic of stimulus and response. Most people will struggle to answer this question because they don't want to admit that whatever $X$ is, it has control over them, but they realize they are in the grip of a recurring pattern. While the person is busy processing this conundrum you can follow up with something like, "Whose anger is it?" To that the response must be, "Mine." And so you can continue with, "So you could choose to be angry or choose another response to this $X$?"

At this point your listener, if you have maintained a caring and supportive manner, will be trying to process his or her choice for another response. And you could state, "I mean, you could choose to be amused, or curious, or just plain bored by $X$ and then you would be free to behave differently, but I guess getting angry is what works for you...."

Now this last statement is a bit bold because you have agreed that the person made the choice to be angry but at the same time shown him or her that there are other choices to respond to the trigger. At this point, the person will either get the awareness and start to take responsibility or will remain lost. If the latter happens, you can model self-leadership by letting the person know how you respond to similar situations; for example: "You know, when this sort of thing happens to me, I remind myself that I am responsible for my own thoughts, feelings, and actions, and that is Me. What other people say or do is Not Me, and so I can choose how I want to respond according to my values and goals."

Once people have taken responsibility *for* their own thoughts, feelings, and actions we can coach them to access confidence (see Chapter 6) and then help them with the self-leadership strategies (Chapter 8), the first of which is improving their belief system.

It has been said that changing people's beliefs against their will is almost impossible, and the authors would agree. If you go head to head with people's beliefs, they will fight you tooth and nail (confirmation bias); however, if you invite them to become aware of what they want and what beliefs are stopping them from reaching that, they may be open to a new frame. Coaches and leaders understand that if we want people to perform or change, they must first believe that it is possible and beneficial for them.

> *"I'm trying to free your mind, Neo. But I can only show you the door. You're the one that has to walk through it."*
> —MORPHEUS IN *The Matrix*, 1999

In his book, *The Secret Language of Leadership*, Stephen Denning states that transformational leaders change the world by generating enthusiasm for a common cause, and they do this by communicating very differently from the traditional mode. Classically, we have been taught to do three things: (1) define the problem, (2) analyze the problem, and (3) recommend action. But this just does not work. If we want to inspire people and create positive change, we must do this instead:

1. Get their attention.

2. Stimulate desire.

3. Reinforce with reasons.

To gain enthusiastic buy-in, leaders need to appeal to the heart as well as the mind, because, as the authors have discovered, people do what they do because of what they think and feel, and what they think and feel is driven by their mental maps and frames of mind.

The most effective way to connect to hearts and minds is through the effective use of stories. The authors have told you many stories throughout this book; we hope we have gotten your attention by letting you know that unless you exercise your self-leadership you are likely to live as a pawn on the chessboard of life. We have told stories about the successful application of self-leadership and how you can positively affect your life, your loved ones, and your organization. And finally we have reinforced these stories with reasons from our research.

To be an effective leader, to influence or suggest a change in the way that people are behaving, we suggest you start your stories where *people* are, not where *you* are. You must connect to their existing scripts and invite them to open a new chapter, to try on a new script. If you paint a picture and invite them to visualize themselves in that picture and to feel all the benefits for them, you will likely reduce resistance to change and maximize the chance of buy-in.

When you are leading as a self-leader, your personal commitment and vision will be influential, but to get people to change how they act, you must communicate in the format we have described.

If you are lucky enough to lead a self-leader or a team of self-leaders, you will have already realized that they do not respond to command-and-control type management (see Chapter 9). So you have to encourage autonomy, self-responsibility, and trust that they will perform. The way to achieve this and maintain a level of accountability is by cocreating goals and through feedback.

A cocreated goal is one that you and your coachee create together through dialogue. Chapter 7 related a series of questions for setting a goal for yourself; these questions form a framework for coaching toward a cocreated goal. The process starts with asking:

- "What do you want to move away from?"

- "What do you want to positively and intentionally achieve or experience?" (desired state)

- "Where are you now?" (present state)

Once you have cocreated a goal with an individual or team and they take responsibility for the action steps, then you can legitimately give supporting feedback to help them stay on track and achieve the goal, which builds their self-confidence and ultimately their self-leadership.

The authors believe that giving feedback is both an art and a science. Before people have achieved a level of self-leadership they are likely to take feedback personally, view it as criticism, and respond defensively. It is therefore important that feedback be delivered with a clear message that you are not judging but simply sharing information that will help the individual to achieve her or his goals.

If you want your feedback to be received and acted upon, you should stick to the facts—what you have observed. You should be able to say, "When I saw this . . ." or, "When I hear you say . . .". Next invite the receiver of the feedback to consider the impact of their action relative to their stated objective, because often people's actions are well intentioned but they lack awareness as to the outcome of their actions. Finally, invite the person or persons to whom you are giving feedback to commit to a future new action that will move them toward their goal.

As an aid to memory, when it comes to feedback, remember FIF: Fact, Impact, Future.

When coauthor Andrew is working with companies to create a high-performing team or self-leadership culture he endeavors to create an acceptance of the frame of mind. Says he: "There is no failure, only feedback for improvement."

## LEADING TEAMS

> *In the new organization the worker is no longer a cog . . .*
> *but is an intelligent part of the overall process.*
> —BILL GATES, 1999

Self-leadership, as mentioned, is actually unselfish and is about finding balance between self and others. Self-leadership includes the ability of each of us to effectively carry his or her own weight, being responsible and responsive, so when it comes to teamwork, self-leadership can mean the difference between successful, rewarding collaborations and difficult, unproductive work.

According to Neck and Houghton (2006), since the late 1980s major leadership authors are arguing that self-leadership among team members is an integral part of the self-managing process (Manz and Sims 1986, 1987, 1994; Manz, 1990). Studies from that period emphasized that the concept of people empowerment was a more productive alternative—teamwise—to the heroic leadership model of the 1970s and 1980s (Conger and Kanungo 1988).

When leading or coaching teams with self-leadership it is essential to establish what behaviors are acceptable and what are not. Bruce Tuckman (1965) called this the "norming" process where norms of behavior are agreed upon.

When conducting workshops with leaders and teams, Andrew conducts an exercise that invites participants to identify which behaviors are above and which are below it (see Figure 11.1). He

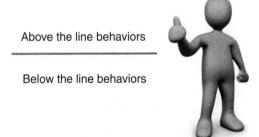

Above the line behaviors

Below the line behaviors

**FIGURE 11.1** Determining What's Above and Below the Line (in Terms of Behavior).

usually starts with punctuality and lateness, which are observable and measurable behaviors that can mean commitment or apathy toward the meeting and other people.

What is interesting about this exercise is that members of a team generally have no problem (with the help of a bit of coaching) agreeing on what behaviors are ideal for high performance, yet they have not been living up to this ideal because those behaviors had not been articulated. Once behavioral norms have been established, the team members can exercise self-leadership to keep their commitments, and the social pressure reinforces this.

Pearce (2004) talked about this is in terms of "team potency." Potency is the collective belief within a team that it can be effective. Potency is a construct between self-efficacy and collective motivation. To create team potency, each member must demonstrate self-leadership.

So how do we create and lead self-leadership teams?

Kouzes and Posner (1987, 1993, 1995) observed more than 1,200 U.S. managers and executives and identified five practices most common in successful leaders:

1. **Challenging processes.** Searching for challenging opportunities, questioning the status quo, experimenting, and taking risks

2. **Inspiring a shared vision.** Envisioning an exciting future and enlisting others (followers and peers) to also see the vision and to pursue that future

3. **Enabling others to act.** Fostering collaboration, and empowering and strengthening followers

4. **Modeling the way.** Consistently practicing the leader's own espoused values, setting an example for how things should be done, and planning incremental accomplishments

5. **Encouraging the heart.** Rewarding good performance, providing positive feedback, recognizing individual contributions, and celebrating team accomplishments.

Leaders' behaviors associated with the practices just mentioned have been positively related to outcomes such as employee motivation, commitment, performance, and retention (Gunter 1997; Herold and Fields 2004; Lowe 2000; McNeese-Smith 1999).

There is plenty of indication that self-leadership enhances teamwork, the same way it does for individual, independent work. A balance, however, needs to be reached so that extreme self-leadership won't jeopardize the very effectiveness it seeks. Recent research is indicating that there is the danger that teams with overly strong self-leadership will lose track of the larger corporation to which they belong.

Millikin, Hom, and Manz (2010) found that when individuals in a team can self-initiate and individually redesign their tasks, their intrinsic motivation will contribute to the team's collective effectiveness. On the other hand, they also found negative effects of low self-control over thoughts and self-statements among team members. Apparently, extremely independent self-managed teams can jeopardize collective performance; extreme individual self-management could hinder the team's focus on the overarching collective mission and integrated efforts of team processes. Extreme self-leaders can go in their own direction, straying from the overall team's goals or from institutional goals. They can also falter in maintaining harmonious relationships throughout their work together.

This study highlights the need for leaders to strengthen team-building activities that create emotional bonds among team members, promote diversity acceptance, encourage collaborative problem solving, and improve conflict management. Even high-performance self-managed teams need leaders to keep them focused on the major collective goals they need to accomplish (e.g., experience enriched tasks), which will result in higher collective potency and purposeful work.

As mentioned in Chapter 9, it is essential to get the right balance between the leader's style and the level of the team's autonomy and responsibility. Many organizations and leaders struggle with the distinction between authority and responsibility. In the old, command-and-control organization, people take no action unless they have been told to do so by an authority figure or are given the authority to act. In a self-leadership culture, people are aligned to the mission, vision, values, and strategic plan and so take responsibility for what needs to be done.

To move a nonperforming team to a high-performing one that demonstrates self-leadership, you need to coach some of the self-leadership principles and strategies such as the style of assertive communication (see Chapter 6) and responsibility *for/to* oneself and others. It is essential that you role-model open and honest communication and encourage all team members to have a voice and be able to listen respectfully to others. This should be one of the line behaviors mentioned previously that everybody agrees to, because in the absence of communication, trust cannot be built or existing trust will be jeopardized.

Andrew once worked with a new pharmaceutical leadership team that was created through merger and acquisition of two existing companies. The members of the new team were half from one company and half from another, all superficially polite but not sharing their concerns or ideas for how they would operate the new business together.

To make this undesirable situation clear to everyone, a behavioral simulation was played where members of the team needed to solve a problem and each member was given a piece of the information required to find the solution. Team members were allowed to share the information but were not to show what was written down and had been given to them. The group was told that people could be allies or adversaries and that adversaries tend to withhold information. If the team suspected a person was behaving as an adversary, that person could be voted off and the information he or she held would be shared with the team as a whole.

What transpired was an initial round of information sharing by the team members. But just having the information was not enough to come up with a solution; some reasoning was required. Instead of reasoning, however, team members just assumed that some people were withholding information, and those people were voted off the team. The team was obviously more focused on completing the task rather than understanding and communicating with team members they didn't trust.

Once the awareness of the lack of trust and communication was established, Andrew was able to coach the team to listen to one another's competencies and build cognitive trust. At the end of the first session, the team created a "Charter of Behaviors" and agreed to be responsible individually and collectively to uphold these behaviors. The top three behaviors on the charter were:

1. Each team member will support and encourage others in the team.

2. Each member will listen to and show respect for other team members.

3. In communication, when unclear what is meant, team members will ask what the intention is rather than asking the more challenging "Why?" question.

Three months later a follow-up session was conducted where team members assessed themselves as to where the team was in terms of performance and where it needed to be. Two key group behaviors were selected from the charter to close the gap in agreed performance. Then each member of the team had five minutes to request of each other member of the team a behavior he or she would like that person to do and modify. Each person was requested to listen carefully to these requests and consider how he or she could integrate the feedback. Some of the requests included:

1. To modify e-mail tone; to move from being conclusive toward being more participative

2. To be more diplomatic in interactions rather than use the current very direct and confrontational style

3. To increase interaction with the peer group rather than work in a "silo" – that is, a business unit that does not collaborate or communicate with other business units

4. To modify current-research and development-only approach and be more open to and collaborative with the business and customer needs

This exercise takes a high degree of trust and self-leadership to be successful, but the payoff is very high in terms of authentic communication and collaboration. In this case, the results have been very powerful: what were once two teams and fourteen people is now one team with one vision and one voice with a positive impact in terms of sales and customer satisfaction.

Most people want to be contributing members in their work environment, seeing it not only as a positive but a necessary role in their personal and professional life (Fairfield 2010). As most of us work in some kind of team, work group, or collaboration, it is essential that we learn how to practice, role-model, and coach self-leadership for a happier and more productive work life. The next chapter shows how the authors' research confirms that self-leadership training or coaching helps people learn and apply self-leadership.

## Summary of the Chapter

Each of us can influence people by being role models or by coaching them to access their own self-leadership. Coaching leads to self-leadership because people have all the resources to solve their own problems. They are much more likely to follow through on a course of action if they come up with the answer themselves. As coaches, we must first get their attention, then stimulate their desire to change, and then we reinforce with reasons. Once someone has taken responsibility *for* his or her own thoughts, feelings, and actions, we can coach that person to access confidence and practice the self-leadership strategies. Leading teams with self-leadership involves the same process as coaching: cocreating goals and processes to get to those goals. Self-leadership is a necessary tool to learn if any of us want to be effective in working with and/or leading teams.

# 12

# Self-Leadership Survey, Toolbox, and What's Next

*There is nothing like returning to a place that remains unchanged to find the ways in which you yourself have altered.*

—NELSON MANDELA

As part of the authors' ongoing dedication to share, teach, and promote self-leadership abilities in ourselves and those around us, we conducted a short survey with volunteer participants in Asia and Australia; the results will be shared with you here. The survey questionnaire we used was the Revised Self-Leadership Questionnaire, by Drs. Jeffrey Houghton and Christopher Neck, which is available to you through the following link at West Virginia University: http://be.wvu.edu/information_technology/survey/surveyHome.htm.

Dr. Houghton and Dr. Neck are well-known self-leadership professors and researchers who authored much of the academic literature we shared with you throughout this book. The West Virginia University research link for the survey is part of an international effort by Dr. Houghton to collect data on self-leadership and study how cultural differences affect it. If you take part in this effort, not only will you be contributing to the study but you will also receive your self-leadership profile analysis, which is a great starting point in your journey to self-knowledge, self-leadership, and leadership.

The survey, conducted while writing this book, was made available to participants of leadership development programs by Andrew Bryant's Self Leadership International company (http://www.selfleadership.com/).

We had 109 participants in this survey, among managers, senior managers, consultants, and individual contributors mainly from Australia (71 percent), of European origin (59 percent), with ages from 23 to 60 years (51 percent up to 36 years old), the majority being females (66 percent), and 52 percent with university degrees. The majority of the respondents (73, or 69.5 percent) were in relationships (married, remarried, or cohabiting), and 83 (79 percent) had self-leadership training, as shown in Table 12.1.

There was no difference in the total self-leadership scores between males and females, between those in or out of relationships, or between people from different countries or with different ethnicities and job positions. Researchers found, however, that having had self-leadership training indeed made a difference both in the total self-leadership score and in the components of this total score. Those who had undergone self-leadership training had higher scores on self–goal setting, self-reward, self-correction, self-observation, natural rewards, visualizing success, and evaluating beliefs. This was a small group to survey, so more research is needed to allow stronger statistical analysis. Nevertheless, this finding brings hope for those of us who want to work on developing our and others' self-leadership. The results signal that indeed we can learn self-leadership—as much as we can learn leadership itself.

**TABLE 12.1** Demographics of the Study's Respondents

| | Frequency | % |
|---|---|---|
| **Gender** | | |
| Female | 69 | 65.7% |
| Male | 36 | 34.3% |
| **Country** | | |
| Australia | 75 | 71.4% |
| Mauritius | 12 | 11.4% |
| Singapore | 6 | 5.7% |
| Others* | 12 | 11.5% |
| **Ethnicity** | | |
| European | 62 | 59.0% |
| Asian | 40 | 38.1% |
| Middle-East and Central/South America | 3 | 2.9% |
| **Education** | | |
| University degree | 55 | 52.4% |
| Secondary education (up to 12 years schooling) | 15 | 14.3% |
| Graduate education – Master's degree | 14 | 13.3% |
| Technical school | 11 | 10.5% |
| Graduate education – MBA | 9 | 8.5% |
| Graduate education – Postdoctorate | 1 | 1.0% |
| **Job position** | | |
| Manager | 32 | 30.5% |
| Individual contributor | 25 | 23.8% |
| Consultant | 20 | 19.0% |
| Supervisor | 11 | 10.5% |
| Senior manager | 10 | 9.5% |
| C-level | 7 | 6.7% |
| **In-Out Relationships** | | |
| In (married, remarried, cohabiting) | 73 | 69.5% |
| Out (single or divorced) | 32 | 30.5% |

*(continued)*

**TABLE 12.1**  Demographics of the Study's Respondents (Continued)

|  | Frequency | % |
|---|---|---|
| **Self-Leadership Training** | | |
| Yes | 83 | 79.0% |
| No | 22 | 21.0% |
| **Age** | | |
| Mean = 30.6 | | |
| Standard deviation = 8.3 | | |
| Minimum = 23 | | |
| Maximum = 60 | | |
| Categories: | | |
| 23–30 years = 27 (25.7%) ⎫ | | |
| 31–40 years = 46 (43.8%) ⎬ Up to 40 years = 73 (69.5%) | | |
| 41–50 years = 26 (24.8%) ⎭ | | |
| 51–60 years = 6 (5.7%) | | |

*Other countries: China, France, Germany, India, Indonesia, Malaysia, Philippines, South Africa, and Thailand.

Past self-leadership studies have shown that there could exist a connection between people's spirituality and self-leadership development and practice (Kazan 1999). Because of that, in this research we asked participants to share their level of spirituality, from "Atheist" to "Religious, practicing," passing through "Spiritual, but not affiliated with a religion" and "Religious, not practicing." While the sample size limits definitive conclusions, the data showed that apparently taking a firm position regarding spirituality—whether to the atheist side or to the practicing religion side—positively impacts a person's self-leadership scores.

Among the respondents in the survey, those who declared themselves to be atheists and those who declared themselves to be practicing religious had the highest scores in total self-leadership;

on its constructs: self-goal setting, self-reward, self-correction, self-observation, self-cueing, and natural rewards; and on the constructive thought pattern strategies: visualizing success, self-talk, and evaluating beliefs. The charts in Figure 12.1 show these findings.

Correlation analysis in this sample showed that total self-leadership scores and its constructs were higher among the older

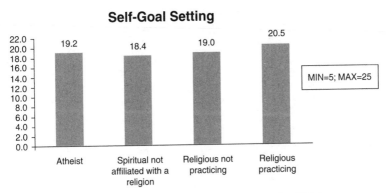

**FIGURE 12.1a**  Practicing religious respondents had higher scores on self-goal setting.

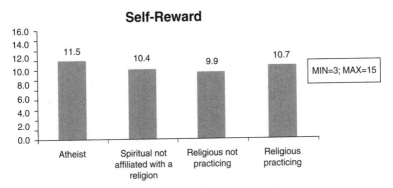

**FIGURE 12.1b**  Atheists scored higher on self-reward practices.

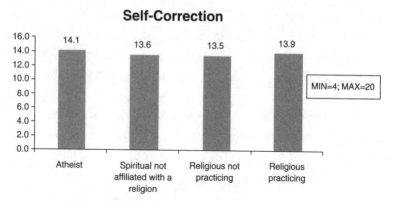

**FIGURE 12.1c** Atheists and practicing religious scored higher on self-correction.

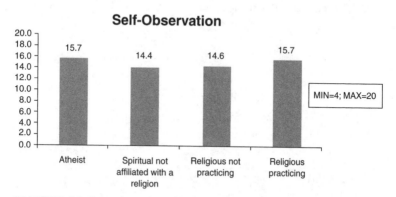

**FIGURE 12.1d** Self-observation is higher among respondents in the extremes of the continuum.

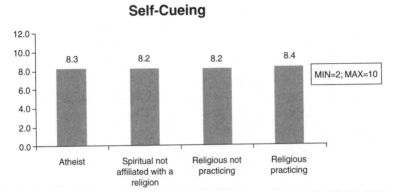

**FIGURE 12.1e** There is little variation in how spirituality impacts self-cueing.

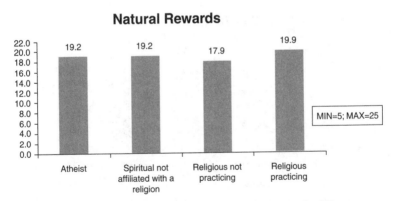

**FIGURE 12.1f** Practicing religious scored higher on building natural rewards in their tasks.

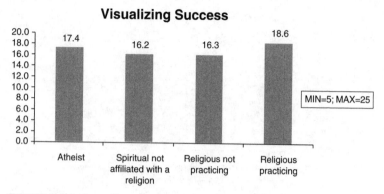

**FIGURE 12.1g**  Practicing religious scored higher on practicing visualizing success.

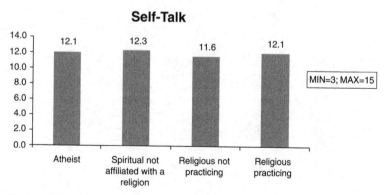

**FIGURE 12.1h**  Nonpracticing religious also don't practice self-talk.

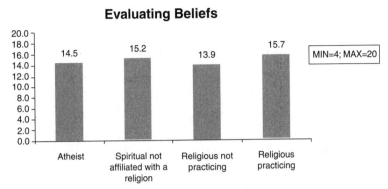

**FIGURE 12.1i** Practicing religious scored higher on evaluating their beliefs.

**FIGURE 12.1j** Practicing religious scored higher on self-leadership.

respondents. This trend held true for both genders in this sample. The authors caution, however, that this was a small sample, and further study is needed to confirm this finding.

The numbers shown in Table 12.2 attest to the significance of the results, even though these were local findings, concerning specifically a few Asian countries and Australia. These findings also give us insight into some of what international research is seeking to find about self-leadership worldwide. Indeed, there are efforts toward clarifying how culture impacts people's understanding and practice of self-leadership, since this concept has been developed and tested mainly in the United States (Neck and Houghton 2006).

It is no wonder that self-leadership is affected by culture, because its aim is self-efficacy through cognitive, behavioral, and mental strategies. These strategies and goals rely heavily on our notions of power, behavior, and influence, concepts that Hofstede (1980) defined as a result of collective mental programming (see also Chapter 9).

In China, a collectivistic culture with performance and humane orientation, high uncertainty avoidance, low assertiveness, and gender egalitarianism, where self is de-emphasized in deference to the group, researchers Neubert and Wu (2006) found that the only component factors in self-leadership that apply to Chinese culture were goal setting, visualizing successful performance, self-talk, self-reward, self-punishment, and natural rewards. The other self-leadership composing factors—self-observation, self-cueing, and evaluating belief and assumptions—couldn't be proven to be strong in the Chinese understanding of self-leadership.

As we explore the self-leadership concept in multicultural settings, it becomes clear that the five cultural dimensions that represent the "fundamental problems of society" (Hofstede 2001, p. 1)—power distance, uncertainty avoidance, individualism/

**TABLE 12.2** Regression Analysis Table: The Impact of Age in Self-Leadership and Its Constructs

| | Self-Goal Setting | Self-Observation | Self-Cueing | Natural Rewards | Visualizing Success | Self-Talk | Evaluating Beliefs | SL TOTAL |
|---|---|---|---|---|---|---|---|---|
| Age | 0.245* | 0.315† | 0.237* | 0.198* | 0.238* | 0.204† | 0.386† | 0.250* |

* $\alpha < 0.05$.
† $\alpha < 0.01$.

collectivism, masculinity/femininity, and future orientation (long-term versus short-term)—manifest themselves differently in every culture (Alves et al. 2006); thus, self-leadership is cultural-dependent. Alves and others (2006) suggested that the different ways in which cultures regard power distance affect self-leadership in terms of the importance of symbolic value to tasks. Those researchers also made the defense that in cultures with high uncertainty avoidance people will make use more often of nonrational, intuition-based thought processes as opposed to the rational thought control proposed by self-leadership. In addition, Alves and others proposed that in more collectivistic cultures people may choose relationships to prevail over the self-reliance proposed by self-leadership.

The authors hope to have stimulated your interest enough to not only have you learning and practicing self-leadership but also participating in the international study being conducted by Dr. Houghton (see the link at the beginning of this chapter).

As stated, the authors firmly believe that self-leadership holds the key for a purposeful life, for mastering all of our thoughts and behaviors, for conducting our lives with decency and responsibility, to become, finally, better human beings.

## WHAT IS NEXT?

In the process of writing this book, the authors realized how much is yet to be said and explored on self-leadership. For instance, work is already underway on the specific impact of self-leadership on women, particularly those of developing countries whose culture strongly restricts the gender's access to education, freedom, and self-expression.

How can self-leadership contribute to improving women's lives everywhere? As a tool for self-efficacy and self-empowerment, self-leadership can serve women who want to revise their lives, their choices, and their attitudes. Self-leadership helps to bring focus and objectivity to whatever struggle they are involved with, harnessing it with direction, organization, meaning, and concerted effort.

The authors believe that all women everywhere can secure their life's accomplishment and have a shot at enduring self-esteem and legitimate personal success. The only way to do so is through the consciousness and responsibility that comes with the practice of self-leadership. Some women do a lot of it naturally, as do some men. But the majority of them definitely do not, as attested to by psychologists and psychiatrists everywhere, who are writing articles to say what happens in their offices when masks are down, defenses are lowered, and the true battered selves of many "monument" women emerge.

Self-leadership can help women to see that it's okay to understand and accept the way things work for each one of us, individually, distinctly, using our best features to overcome our own personal challenges. Self-leadership gets people going and gives them the endurance to try again and again until they have it all right or figured out. It eliminates the waiting for someone else to take care of our lives, and instead puts us in the "driver's seat" en route to take care of our own lives. Self-leadership helps us listen to ourselves, understand what we really want, and know what really makes us happy beyond image and externalities. It makes us better, more beautiful, and more complete, both inside and outside.

There is nothing as attractive for women as a combination of clean attitude, internal beauty, and external beauty. No matter at what age—young or old—inner peace is unbeatable as a beauty treatment.

The authors are also developing work on how self-leadership education impacts children and can bring them to become fulfilled, concerned, and engaged adults to face the demands of our future.

For example, coauthor Andrew has his toddlers (five and six years old) studying at United World College of South East Asia where the principles of their Primary Years Program promote self-leadership. Rachel Lewis, Andrew's five-year-old son's kindergarten teacher, shared some of these principles:

1. Every child has strengths in areas apart from the traditional academic ones—sports, drama, music, visual art, information technologies, creativity, empathy, and so on. Every area is equally important and should be given time and attention.

2. Children are not empty vessels or sponges that come to receive information from the teacher. They are valued for their ideas and thoughts. Children are naturally very creative and often great lateral thinkers. Give them opportunities to say what their ideas are and to test hypotheses. Through group meetings and discussions, they can come up with their own projects and decide together (with some facilitation from the teacher) how they will carry that out.

3. Children should be given access to all the resources they need, and at United World College classrooms are organized so that the children can find and use paper, computers, books, cameras, and so on so that they can try out different things and follow through with their ideas.

4. Sometimes the end result of a self-initiated project does not look as "pretty" as one that the teacher has done, but there is a lot more thought and skill involved in the process. It's important that children are making decisions, solving problems, and trying things out for themselves. When we value these kinds of artwork by talking about it and displaying it, we are giving the children the message that their ideas are valued.

5. Children have the ability and capacity to discover things for themselves, and this is the best way they will learn, because they are not being passive—they are actively making connections and solving problems.

6. Metacognition, the ability to think about one's own thinking and learning, is extremely important, because we need to be able to monitor ourselves to become good learners. Teachers at United World College do such things as ask the children what color their brain feels like today.

Some very important skills, which will become increasingly important as the world changes are communication, group work, generating ideas, solving problems, analyzing, categorizing, researching, and synthesizing. Doesn't it make sense that we equip children with these skills?

Andrew is very proud that his children are already able to distinguish "I have to" from "I choose to" and that they are learning to respect others and take responsibility for their thoughts and actions.

Self-leadership is a daily journey, a daily choice, and a lifelong learning. The authors passionately embrace it and hope to have engaged you throughout this book to embrace it as well.

## YOUR TOOLBOX

As you start your own self-leadership journey, keep in mind some of the major points about this liberating practice, so that your route can be easier:

1. **Observe yourself.** It's your life, not someone else's. Focus first on what you need to do to improve yourself, and work from this perspective forward. Do whatever it takes

to get to know this wonderful person that you are, with all the perfections and imperfections that make you human, and work with this canvas to accept it, improve it, complement it, and grant it a good ride this life.

2. **Consider and reconsider the beliefs that are running you.** It could be that you are holding onto beliefs about yourself and the world that are no longer true. Make sure that you will recheck for validity all those automatic thoughts that guide your actions and behaviors, and commit to change them if you realize that they are not applicable anymore to the person you are now or want to be.

3. **Practice imagination.** Place yourself where you want to be, rehearse desirable behaviors, practice self-talk, and encourage yourself as you would with any best friend. Practice in yourself the courage and initiative you always try to instill in your friends. Be bold about your own destiny.

4. **Correct and reward yourself.** As you would with a child or a good friend, celebrate reaching your benchmarks, correct your route when you feel you strained, and be the master of your life. The power is with you, not with anyone else.

5. **Surround yourself with your likes.** If you want to be an eagle, don't fly around with crows. If you want to improve your life, make sure that you surround yourself with all the elements that will conduct you to your goal. If you want to study and learn new skills, you will need discipline, so hanging around with late-nighters won't help. Everything that happens to you from this point on is your responsibility, your merit, and your fault. You cannot blame anyone else. It's all about you now.

6. **Be prepared to make this decision—of being responsible for your life—every day.** Every day will bring a dif-

ferent challenge, a different request from life, and you can always choose to either let go of your own control or do the best you can to face it and handle it with the responsibility it needs. The authors guarantee you that the effort is all worthwhile!

The authors welcome your impressions and feedback. Please write to us (analuciakazan@gmail.com or andrew.bryant@ selfleadership.com) and let us know how this book has changed you, what you plan to work on, and what else you would like to see regarding self-leadership. Both of us—Andrew and Ana—are committed to living self-leadership in our lives and to spreading to the world around us how we experience the benefits that its daily practice have added to our lives.

Have a good journey!

## Summary of the Chapter

In this chapter we share the results of a survey we conducted while writing this book, with 109 professionals from Asia and Australia, all former participants of coauthor Andrew's personal/ organizational improvement programs. We wanted to see whether there would be differences in self-leadership scores—and its constructs—within this sample, based on gender, age, marital status, ethnicity, country, spirituality, and former self-leadership training.

We found no difference in self-leadership scores of males and females, or in the scores of people in and out of relationships. Nor did we find differences based on country or origin, ethnicity, or job position. We found, however, higher scores for those who have undergone self-leadership training, not only on the total questionnaire score, but also on the constructs associated with self-leadership: self–goal setting, self-reward, self-correction, self-observation, natural rewards, visualizing success, and evaluating beliefs. Although more research is needed to strengthen these results, these findings show that we can indeed learn self-leadership as much as we can learn leadership itself.

# References

## CHAPTER 2

Bandura, A. (1971). *Social learning theory.* Morristown, NJ: General Learning Press.

Bandura, A. (1977). *Social learning theory.* New York: General Learning Press.

Bandura, A. (1986). *Social foundations of thought and action: A social cognitive theory.* Englewood Cliffs, NJ: Prentice-Hall.

Benabou, R., & Tirole, J. (2002). Self-confidence and personal motivation. *The Quarterly Journal of Economics, 117*(3), 871–915.

Block, J. H., & Block, J. (1980). The role of ego-control and ego-resiliency in the origination of behavior. In W. A. Collings (Ed.), *The Minnesota Symposia on Child Psychology* (Vol. 13, pp. 39–101). Hillsdale, NJ: Erlbaum.

Block, J., & Kremen, A. M. (1996). IQ and ego-resiliency: Conceptual and empirical connections and separateness. *Journal of Personality and Social Psychology, 70* (2), 349–361.

Burns, D. D. (1980). *Feeling good: The new mood therapy.* New York: New American Library.

Darley, J. M., & Latané, B. (1969). Bystander "apathy." *American Scientist, 57,* 244–268.

Deci, E. L., & Ryan, R. M. (1985). Intrinsic motivation and self-determination in human behavior. New York: Plenum Press.

Edic, M. (1997). *Self-motivation and the self-employed: Keep your passion alive and achieve your goals.* Rocklin, CA: Prima Publishers.

Gardner, W. I., & Cole, C. L. (1988). Self-monitoring procedures. In E. S. Shapiro & T. R. Kratochwoll (Eds.), *Behavioral assessment in schools* (pp. 206–246). New York: Guilford Press.

Hornby, A. S., & Ruse, C. A. (1986). *Oxford dictionary.* New York: Oxford University Press.

Lazarus, R. S. (1993a). Coping theory and research: Past, present, and future. *Psychosomatic Medicine, 55*, 234–247.

Lazarus, R. S. (1993b). From psychological stress to the emotions: A history of changing outlooks. *Annual Review of Psychology, 44*, 1–21.

Manz, C. C. (1986). Self-leadership: Toward an expand theory of self-influence processes in organizations. *Academy of Management Review, 11*(3), 586–600.

Rotter, J. B. (1954). *Social learning and clinical psychology.* New York: Prentice-Hall.

Sears, P. A. (1990). *An attribution theory of self-confidence.* Unpublished Doctoral Dissertation. Cleveland, OH: Case Western University.

Snyder, M. (1974). Self-monitoring of expressive behavior. *Journal of Personality and Social Psychology, 30*, 526–537.

Snyder, M. (1979). Self-monitoring processes. In L. Berkowitz (Ed.), *Advances in experimental social psychology, 12* (pp. 86–128). New York: Academic Press.

Soloman, L. Z., Solomon, H., & Stone, R. (1978). Helping as a function of number of bystanders and ambiguity of emergency. *Personality and Social Psychology Bulletin, 4*, 318–321.

Spitzer, D. R. (1995). *Supermotivation: A blueprint for energizing your organization from top to bottom.* New York: American Management Association.

Tugade, M. M., Fredrickson, B. L., & Barrett, L. F. (2006). Psychological resilience and positive emotional granularity: Examining the benefits of positive emotions on coping and health. *Journal of Personal Psychology, 72*(6), 1161–1190.

## CHAPTER 3

Covey, S. R. (2004). *The seven habits of highly effective people.* New York: Free Press.

Frankl, V. E. (2004). *On the theory and therapy of mental disorders: An introduction to logotherapy and existential analysis.* London-New York: Brunner-Routledge.

Hall, L. M. (2011). *Secrets of personal mastery.* Carmarthen, UK: Crown House Publishing.

Mahler, M. S., Pine, F., & Bergman, A. (1975, 2000). *The psychological birth of the human infant: Symbiosis and individuation.* New York: Basic Books.

Pavlov, I. P. (1927). *Conditioned reflexes.* London: Oxford University Press.

Siegel, D. (1999). *The developing mind: How relationships and the brain interact to shape who we are.* New York: Guilford Press.

### CHAPTER 4

Bandura, A. (1977). *Social learning theory.* Englewood Cliffs, NJ: Prentice-Hall.

Hall, M. L. (2003). *Games business experts play.* Carmarthen, UK: Crown House Publishing.

Kenrick, D. T., Griskevicius, V., Neuberg, S. L., & Schaller, M. (2010). Renovating the pyramid of needs: Contemporary extensions built upon ancient foundations. *Perspectives on Psychological Science, 5*(3), 292–314.

Maslow, A. H. (1943). A theory of human motivation. *Psychological Review 50*(4), 370–396.

Rogers, E. (1995). *Diffusion of innovations* (4th ed.). New York: The Free Press.

Williams, K. D. (2007). Ostracism. *Annual Review of Psychology, 58*(1), 425–452.

### CHAPTER 5

Ferriss, T. (2009). *The 4-hour workweek.* Carmarthen, UK: Crown House Publishing.

Jobs, S. (2005). "You've got to find what you love." Commencement address delivered by Steve Jobs, CEO of Apple Computer and of Pixar Animation Studios, on June 12, 2005, at Stanford University. Available online: http://news.stanford.edu/news/2005/june15/jobs-061505.html (accessed April 6, 2012).

Kouzes, J. M., & Posner, B. Z. (2002). *The leadership challenge.* Hoboken. NJ: John Wiley & Sons.

Lyubomirsky, S. (2007). *The how of happiness.* London, England: Penguin Books.

Niedenthal, P. M., Krauth-Gruber, S., & Ric, F. (2006). *Psychology of emotion: Interpersonal, experimental, and cognitive approaches* (pp. 5, 305–342). New York: Psychology Press.

Robin, V., & Dominguez, J. (1999). *Your money or your life.* London, England: Penguin Books.

## CHAPTER 6

Baldwin, N. (2001). *Edison: Inventing the century.* Chicago: The University of Chicago Press.

Bandura, A. (1977). *Social learning theory.* Englewood Cliffs, NJ: Prentice-Hall.

Berlo, D. K. (1979). *The process of communication.* New York: Holt, Rinehart and Winston, Inc.

Berlo, D. K. (2003). *O processo da comunicação: Introdução à teoria e prática* (10th ed.). Sao Paulo, Brasil: Editora Martins Fontes.

Bodenhamer, B. G., & Hall, L. M. (2000). *The user's manual for the brain.* Carmarthen, UK: Crown House Publishing.

Davenport, T., & Beck, J. (2000). Getting attention when you need. *Harvard Business Review, Sept.–Oct. 2000,* 118–126.

Eisenberger, N., Lieberman, M., & Williams, K. D. (2003). Does rejection hurt? An fMRI study of social exclusion. *Science, 302* (5643), 290–292.

Jordan, M. From http://www.amazon.com/Cant-Accept-Not-Trying-Excellence/dp/0062511904/ref=sr_1_5?ie=UTF8&qid=1333859360 &sr=8-5; quoted in http://www.brainyquote.com/quotes/quotes/m/michaeljor127660.html.

Khoo, K.-H., (2002). *Applying Sun Tzu's Art of War in Winning.* Subang Jaya, Malaysia: Pelanduk Publications.

Lieberman, M., & Eisenberger, N. (2009). The pains and pleasures of social life. *Science, 323*(5916), 890–891.

Rosenberg, M. B. (2003). *Nonviolent communication.* Encinitas, CA: Puddle-Dancer Press.

Rosenthal, R., & Jacobson, L. (1992). *Pygmalion in the classroom: Teacher expectation and pupils' intellectual development.* New York: Irvington Publishers.

Tzu, S. (2007). *The art of war.* (Samuel B. Griffith, trans.). New York: Oxford University Press.

## CHAPTER 7

Bandler, R., & Grinder, J. (1975a). *The structure of magic I: A book about language and therapy.* Palo Alto, CA: Science & Behavior Books.

Bandler, R., & Grinder, J. (1975b). *The structure of magic II: A book about communication and change.* Palo Alto, CA: Science & Behavior Books.

Cameron-Bandler, L. (1986). *The emotional hostage: Rescuing your emotional life*. Boulder, CO: Real People Press.

Covey, S. (2004). *The seven habits of highly effective people*. New York: Free Press.

Hall, L. M., & Bodenhamer, B. G. (1997/2000). *Figuring out people: Reading people using meta-programs*. Williston, VT: Crown House Publishing, Ltd. http://www.amazon.com/Figuring-Out-People-Reading-Meta-Programs/dp/1899836101.

Myers, I. B., McCaulley, M. H., Quenk, N. L., & Hammer, A. L. (1998). *MBTI manual: A guide to the development and use of the Myers-Briggs Type Indicator* (3rd ed.). Palo Alto, CA: Consulting Psychologists Press, Inc.

Niemiec, R. M. (2009). Strengths spotting worksheet. Workshop materials, VIA Institute on Character.

Peterson, C., & Seligman, M. E. (2004). *Character strengths and virtues: A handbook and classification*. New York: Oxford University Press.

Seligman, M. E. (2003). *Authentic happiness*. Boston, MA: Nicholas Brealey Publishing.

## CHAPTER 8

Bandler, R. (1985). Using your brain for a change: Neuro-linguistic programming. Boulder, CO: Real People Press.

Briñol, P., Petty, R. E., & Wagner, B. (2009). Body posture effects on self-evaluation: A self-validation approach. *European Journal of Social Psychology, 39*, 1053–1064.

Deci, E. L., & Ryan, R. M. (1985). *Intrinsic motivation and self-determination in human behavior*. New York: Plenum.

Frankl, V. (1963). *Man's search for meaning*. New York: Washington Square Press, Simon and Schuster.

Hill, N. (1960). *Think and grow rich*. New York: Fawcett Books.

Khoo, K.-H. (2002). *Applying Sun Tzu's art of war in winning*. Subang Jaya, Malaysia: Pelanduk Publications.

Manz, C. C. (1983). Improving performance through self-leadership. *National Productivity Review, 207*, Summer.

Manz, C. C. (1986). Self-leadership: Towards an expanded theory of self-influence processes in organizations. *Academy of Management Review, 11*(3), 585–600.

Manz, C. C. (1990a). The art of self-leadership. *Executive Excellence, 7* (8), 7–8.

Manz, C. C. (1990b). Beyond self-managing teams: Toward self-leading teams in the workplace. In R. Woodman & W. Pastore (Eds.), *Research in organizational change and development* (pp. 273–299). Greenwich, CT: JAI Press.

Manz, C. C. (1990c). Beyond self-managing teams: Toward self-leading teams in the workplace. *Organizational Change and Development, 4,* 273–299.

Manz, C. C. (1991). Helping yourself and others to master self-leadership. *Getting Results for the Hands-On Manager, 36*(11), 8–9.

Manz, C. C. (1992). Self-leadership . . . the heart of empowerment. *Journal for Quality and Participation,* July/August, 80–84.

Manz, C. C., Mossholder, K. W., & Luthans, F. (1987). An integrated perspective of self-control in organizations. *Administration and Society, 19*(1), 3–24.

Manz, C. C., & Neck, C. P. (1991). Inner leadership: Creating productive thought patterns. *Academy of Management Executive, 5*(3), 87–95.

Manz, C. C., & Neck, C. P. (1992). Thought self-leadership: The influence of self-talk and mental imagery on performance. *Journal of Organizational Behavior, 13,* 681–699.

Manz, C. C., & Neck, C. P. (1999). *Mastering self-leadership: Empowering yourself for personal excellence.* Upper Saddle River, NJ: Prentice Hall.

Manz, C. C., & Neck, C. P. (2004). *Mastering self-leadership: Empowering yourself for personal excellence,* 3rd edition, Upper Saddle River, NJ: Pearson Prentice Hall.

Manz, C. C., & Sims, H. P. (1980). Self management as a substitute for leadership: A social learning theory perspective. *Academy of Management Review, 5*(3), 361–367.

Manz, C. C., & Sims, H. P. (1989). *Super-leadership.* Englewood Cliffs, NJ: Prentice Hall.

Manz, C. C., & Sims, H. P. (1991). Superleadership: Beyond the myth of heroic leadership. *Organizational Dynamics, 19,* 18–35.

Manz, C. C., & Sims, H. P. (1997). Superleadership: Beyond the myth of heroic leadership. In R. P. Vecchio (Ed.), *Leadership: Understanding the dynamics of power and influence in organizations* (pp. 411–421). South Bend, IN: University of Notre Dame Press.

Neck, C. P., & Houghton, J. D. (2006). Two decades of self-leadership theory and research: Past developments, present trends, and future possibilities. *Journal of Managerial Psychology, 21*(4), 270–295.

Neck, C. P., & Manz, C. C. (1996a). Thought self-leadership: The impact of mental strategies on employee cognition, behavior, and affect. *Journal of Organizational Behavior, 17*, 445–467.

Neck, C. P., & Manz, C. C. (1996b). Total leadership quality: Integrating employee self-leadership and total quality management. *Advances in the Management of Organizational Quality, 1*, 39–77.

Norris, S. E. (2008). An examination of self-leadership. *Emerging Leadership Journeys, 1*(2), 43–61.

Pollard, J. K. (1992). *The self-parenting program: Core guidelines for the self-parenting practitioner.* Malibu, CA: Generic Human Studies Publishing.

Prussia, G. E., Anderson, J. S., & Manz, C. C. (1998). Self-leadership and performance outcomes: The mediating influence of self-efficacy. *Journal of Organizational Behavior, 19*, 523–538.

Rokeach, M. (1960). *Open and closed minds.* New York: Basic Books.

## CHAPTER 9

Adler, N. J. (1997). Global leadership: Women leaders. *Management International Review, 37*(1), 171–196.

Alves, J. C., Lovelace, K. J., Manz, C. C., Matsypura, D., Toyasaki, F., and Ke, K. (2006). A cross-cultural perspective of self-leadership. *Journal of Managerial Psychology, 21*(4), 338–359.

Chaijukul, Y. (2010). An examination of self-leadership performance mechanism model in Thai Private Organization. *The Journal of Behavioral Science, 5*(1), 15–32.

Curral, L., & Marques-Quinteiro, P. (2009). Autoliderazgo y motivación de rol laboral: Prueba de un modelo de mediación con orientación de meta y orientación laboral (Self-leadership and work role innovation: Testing a mediation model with goal orientation and work motivation). *Revista de Psicología del Trabajo y de las Organizaciones, 25*(2), 165–176.

Ho, J., & Nesbitt, P. L. (2008). A refinement and extension of the self-leadership scale for the Chinese context. *Journal of Managerial Psychology, 24*(5), 450–476.

Hofstede, G. (2001). *Culture's consequences: Comparing values, behaviors, institutions, and organizations across nations* (2nd ed.). Thousand Oaks, CA: Sage Publications.

Kazan, A. L., Moore, M., Jones, J. M., & Safrit, R. D. (1998). *Not male, nor female: Androgynous is the new style for managers and leaders.* Lincolnshire, United Kingdom: Fifth Annual International Conference on Advances in Management, July 8–11.

Revans, R. W. (1980). *Action learning: New techniques for management.* London: Blond & Briggs, Ltd.

Revans, R. W. (1982). *The origin and growth of action learning.* Brickley, UK: Chartwell-Bratt.

Revans, R. W. (1998). *ABC of action learning.* London, UK: Lemos and Crane.

Wollard, K. K. (2011). Quiet desperation: Another perspective on employee engagement. *Advances in Developing Human Resources, 20*(10), 1–12.

## CHAPTER 10

Drath, W. H. (2008). Leadership beyond leaders and followers. *Leadership in Action, 28*(5). Hoboken, NJ: John Wiley & Sons.

Dutton, J. E., Glynn, M. A., & Spreitzer, G. (2006). Positive organizational scholarship. *Michigan Ross School of Business Working Paper Series.* Center for Positive Organizational Scholarship, Ann Arbor, MI. Available at: http://www.bus.umich.edu/Positive/PDF/Dutton-POS-Encyc-of-Career-Devel.pdf (accessed 10/21/2011).

Kazan, A. L. (1999). *Exploring the concept of self-leadership: Factors impacting self-leadership of Ohio americorps members.* Unpublished Doctoral Dissertation. Columbus, OH: The Ohio State University.

Marques, J. (Ed.). (2009). *The workplace and spirituality: New perspectives in research and practice.* Woodstock, VT: SkyLight Paths Publishing.

Marques, J. (2010). Awakened leaders: Who are they and why do we need them? *Development and Learning in Organizations, 24*(2), 7–10.

McEwen, W. J. (2011). Planning for the new normal. In G. Brewer and B. Sanford (Eds.), *Decade of change* (pp. 204–208). New York: Gallup Press.

Poppo, Laura, Zhou, Kevin Zheng, and Rhu, Sungmin (2007). Alternative Origins to Interorganizational Trust: An Interdependence Perspective on the Shadow of the Past and the Shadow of the Future (January 2007). Available at SSRN: http://ssrn.com/abstract=975472.

Singer, P. (1995). *How are we to live? Ethics in an age of self-interest.* Amherst, NY: Prometheus Books.

Smyth, P. (2010). *The wind that calls out my name.* Aging, Spirituality and Health Conference. The Council on Aging of Ottawa, ON. Available at http://www.coaottawa.ca/news-events/events/documents/DrPhyllis Smythpresentation.pdf (accessed 10/21/2011).

## CHAPTER 11

Conger, J., & Kanungo, R. (1988). The empowerment process: Integrating theory and practice. *The Academy of Management Review, 13,* 639–652.

Davis, M. (2007). *Sanctified emotions.* Retrieved from http://www.livingwords. net/wp-content/uploads/2011/02/Sanctified-Emotions-e-book.pdf.

Denning, S. (2007). *The secret language of leadership: How leaders inspire action.* San Francisco, CA: Jossey-Bass.

Fairfield, K. D. (2010). Growing up and growing out: Emerging adults learn management through service-learning. *Journal of Management Education, 34* (1), 113–141.

Gunter, D. M. (1997). *Leadership practices and organizational commitment.* Unpublished doctoral dissertation, Nova Southeastern University.

Herold, D., & Fields, D. (2004). Making sense of subordinate feedback for leadership development: Confounding effects of job role and organizational rewards. *Group and Organization Management 29*(6), 686–701.

Kouzes, J. M., & Posner, B. Z. (1987). *The leadership challenge,* 2nd edition, San Francisco, CA: Jossey-Bass.

Kouzes, J. M., & Posner, B. Z. (1993). Psychometric properties of the leadership practices inventory—updated. *Educational and Psychological Measurement, 53,* 191–199.

Kouzes, J. M., & Posner, B. Z. (1995). *The leadership challenge,* 2nd edition, San Francisco, CA: Jossey-Bass.

Lowe, W. A. (2000). *An examination of the relationship between leadership practices and organizational commitment in the fire service.* Unpublished doctoral dissertation, Nova Southeastern University.

Manz, C. C. (1990). How to become a SuperLeader. *Executive Excellence, 7*(6), 10–13.

Manz, C. C., & Sims, H. P., Jr. (1986). Leading self-managed groups: A conceptual analysis of a paradox. *Economic and Industrial Democracy, 7,* 141–165.

Manz, C. C., & Sims, H. P., Jr. (1987). Leading workers to lead themselves: The external leadership of self-managing work teams. *Administrative Science Quarterly, 32,* 106–128.

Manz, C. C., & Sims, H. P., Jr. (1994). *Business without bosses: How self-managing work teams are building high-performing companies.* New York: John Wiley & Sons.

McNeese-Smith, D. K. (1999). The relationship between managerial motivation, leadership, nurse outcomes, and patient satisfaction. *Journal of Organizational Behavior, 20,* 243–259.

Millikin, J. P., Hom, P. W., & Manz, C. C. (2010). Self-management competencies in self-managing teams: Their impact on multi-team system productivity. *The Leadership Quarterly, 21,* 687–702.

Neck, C. P., & Houghton, J. D. (2006). Two decades of self-leadership theory and research: Past developments, present trends, and future possibilities. *Journal of Managerial Psychology, 21*(4), 270–295.

Pearce, C. L. (2004). The future of leadership: Combining vertical and shared leadership to transform knowledge work. *Academy of Management Executives, 18*(1), 47–57.

Tuckman, Bruce W. (1965). Developmental sequence in small groups. *Psychological Bulletin, 63,* 384–399. The article was reprinted in *Group Facilitation: A Research and Applications Journal,* Number 3, Spring 2001, and is available as a Word document: http://dennislearningcenter.osu.edu/references/GROUP%20DEV%20ARTICLE.doc (accessed 12/20/2011).

## CHAPTER 12

Alves, J. C., Lovelace, K. J., Manz, C. C., Matsypura, D., Toyasaki, F., & Ke, K. (2006). A cross-cultural perspective on self-leadership. *Journal of Managerial Psychology, 21*(4), 338–359.

Hofstede, G. (1983). The cultural relativity of organizational practices and theories. *Journal of International Business Studies, 14* (2), 75–89.

Hofstede, G. (1997). *Cultures and organizations: Software of the mind: Intercultural cooperation and its impact for survival.* New York: McGraw-Hill.

Hofstede, G. (2001). *Culture's consequences: Comparing values, behaviors, institutions, and organizations across nations* (2nd ed.). Thousand Oaks, CA: Sage Publications.

Neck, C. P., & Houghton, J. D. (2006). Two decades of self-leadership theory and research: Past developments, present trends, and future possibilities. *Journal of Managerial Psychology, 21*(4), 270–295.

Neubert, M. J., & Wu, J. C. (2006). An investigation of the generalizability of the Houghton and Neck Revised Self-Leadership Questionnaire to a Chinese context. *Journal of Managerial Psychology, 21*(4), 360–373.

# Index

# About the Authors

**Andrew Bryant**

As a globally recognized thought leader on self-leadership and leading people, Andrew Bryant is highly sought after for his ability to inspire people to question conventional wisdom and take actions that result in positive outcomes. His unique presentation style blends constructive realism with humor to entertain and engage audiences worldwide.

Andrew has extensive experience as a consultant and executive coach to senior leaders and leadership teams across the world. His client list includes such companies as Microsoft, Nokia, Credit Suisse, Hess, Deutsche Bank, Merck, and Sennheisser.

He is the founder of Self Leadership International, a provider of leadership and people development solutions including consulting, coaching, facilitation, and training.

For more information on self-leadership solutions go to www.selfleadership.com and read his blog at www.selfleadership.com/blog.

Andrew Bryant is a Certified Professional Speaker and is in demand worldwide as an inspirational conference speaker and facilitator. For more information on Andrew and the latest tips and tools go to www.andrew-bryant.com and subscribe to his tweets @selfleadership.

## Ana Lucia Kazan, Ph.D.

A native of Brazil and an international scholar, Dr. Kazan has taught and conducted research both in Brazil and in the United States, with The Ohio State University (OSU), Ohio Department of Development, Nationwide Enterprise, North Carolina State University (NCSU), São Paulo State Research Foundation (FAPESP), Institute for Management Teaching and Research (INEPAD), Universidade Metodista (UNIMEP), Universidade Paulista (UNIP), and Universidade de São Paulo (USP) School of Medicine in Ribeirão Preto, Brazil. As a former journalist, she has published extensively both as a reporter and as an editor, at O Estado de São Paulo and Jornal de Piracicaba, besides other local newspapers, radio, and TV media.

Dr. Kazan holds a masters and a doctorate degree from OSU, and her work toward spreading the message of self-leadership in Brazil has brought her to speak to audiences of hundreds of executives through the American Chamber of Commerce in Brazil (Ribeirao Preto), through Livraria Cultura and Universidade de Ribeirão Preto (UNAERP).

At the time of the publication of this book, Dr. Kazan is finishing her postdoctoral research with NCSU while developing new approaches to research and data analysis with the Brazilian National Institute for Geography and Statistics (IBGE).

Her continued interest in self-leadership and personal improvement brings her opportunites to speak publicly almost continuously, as well as to publish lay and academic articles in both Brazilian and international media. She can be contacted by e-mail at analuciakazan@gmail.com.